Social and cultural impacts of tourism

Klara Böhm

Social and cultural impacts of tourism

A holistic management approach for sustainable development

VDM Verlag Dr. Müller

Impressum/Imprint (nur für Deutschland/ only for Germany)
Bibliografische Information der Deutschen Nationalbibliothek: Die Deutsche Nationalbibliothek verzeichnet diese Publikation in der Deutschen Nationalbibliografie; detaillierte bibliografische Daten sind im Internet über http://dnb.d-nb.de abrufbar.
Alle in diesem Buch genannten Marken und Produktnamen unterliegen warenzeichen-, marken- oder patentrechtlichem Schutz bzw. sind Warenzeichen oder eingetragene Warenzeichen der jeweiligen Inhaber. Die Wiedergabe von Marken, Produktnamen, Gebrauchsnamen, Handelsnamen, Warenbezeichnungen u.s.w. in diesem Werk berechtigt auch ohne besondere Kennzeichnung nicht zu der Annahme, dass solche Namen im Sinne der Warenzeichen- und Markenschutzgesetzgebung als frei zu betrachten wären und daher von jedermann benutzt werden dürften.

Coverbild: www.purestockx.com

Verlag: VDM Verlag Dr. Müller Aktiengesellschaft & Co. KG
Dudweiler Landstr. 99, 66123 Saarbrücken, Deutschland
Telefon +49 681 9100-698, Telefax +49 681 9100-988, Email: info@vdm-verlag.de

Herstellung in Deutschland:
Schaltungsdienst Lange o.H.G., Berlin
Books on Demand GmbH, Norderstedt
Reha GmbH, Saarbrücken
Amazon Distribution GmbH, Leipzig
ISBN: 978-3-639-13471-1

Imprint (only for USA, GB)
Bibliographic information published by the Deutsche Nationalbibliothek: The Deutsche Nationalbibliothek lists this publication in the Deutsche Nationalbibliografie; detailed bibliographic data are available in the Internet at http://dnb.d-nb.de.
Any brand names and product names mentioned in this book are subject to trademark, brand or patent protection and are trademarks or registered trademarks of their respective holders. The use of brand names, product names, common names, trade names, product descriptions etc. even without a particular marking in this works is in no way to be construed to mean that such names may be regarded as unrestricted in respect of trademark and brand protection legislation and could thus be used by anyone.

Cover image: www.purestockx.com

Publisher:
VDM Verlag Dr. Müller Aktiengesellschaft & Co. KG
Dudweiler Landstr. 99, 66123 Saarbrücken, Germany
Phone +49 681 9100-698, Fax +49 681 9100-988, Email: info@vdm-verlag.de

Copyright © 2009 by the author and VDM Verlag Dr. Müller Aktiengesellschaft & Co. KG and licensors
All rights reserved. Saarbrücken 2009

Printed in the U.S.A.
Printed in the U.K. by (see last page)
ISBN: 978-3-639-13471-1

TABLE OF CONTENTS

TABLE OF CONTENTS 1

1 INTRODUCTION 3

2 CREATING A FRAMEWORK 7
   2.1 An attempt to draw lines between the concepts of ecotourism, rural tourism and sustainable development 7
   2.2 A common issue - cultural and social aspects 14

3 SOCIAL AND CULTURAL ASPECTS OF TOURISM 16
   3.1 Culture and cultural aspects of tourism 18
   3.2 Society and social aspects 26
   3.3 Factors influencing the social and cultural impacts 30
   3.4 Difficulties to measure social and cultural impacts 32

4 QUALITY MANAGEMENT IN TOURISM 34
   4.1 Concept of Quality 34
   4.2 Measurement of Quality 37
   4.3 Quality Management 38

5 THE INTEGRATION OF SOCIAL AND CULTURAL ASPECTS IN A QUALITY MANAGEMENT SYSTEM 45
   5.1 Impact assessment models 47
   5.2 Management and planning tools for tourism impacts 55
   5.3 Controlling and Monitoring 78

6 LA GOMERA 81
   6.1 Rural Tourism on the Canary Islands 82
   6.2 Development of tourism on La Gomera 83
   6.3 Resource diagnosis 90
   6.4 Set of sustainability indicators 95
   6.5 Tourism Players on La Gomera 108
   6.6 SWOT Analysis of Rural Tourism on La Gomera 110

7 SUGGESTIONS FOR ACTION 116
   7.1 The importance of the individual players in tourism 117
   7.2 New forms of cooperation 122

8 FINAL CONCLUSIONS 126

TABLE OF ABBREVIATIONS 130

BIBLIOGRAPHY 131

1 INTRODUCTION

"The world, clearly, is not going to stop taking holidays – but equally clearly we can no longer afford to ignore the consequences." (Page, Dowling, 2002, 148) Today tourism is one of the leading industries worldwide. Many regions, especially small island destinations, are often economically dependent on the tourism industry. Nevertheless, many examples all over the world have shown that tourism can not be regarded as a last resort for an economic upturn without negative side effects. The consequences of tourism have long been acknowledged but in many cases economic interests have hindered any remedial action. The right to travel has implicitly become a human right, but at the same time responsibility has to be accepted from the part of the tourists, the local residents and all tourism players.

"In the European tradition, culture has from the outset been part of the essence of tourism. Even so, it is not in most instances the explicit goal but a pretext that legitimises a recreational experience. Tourism is an opportunity for culture, but at the same time it consumes, contaminates and ultimately can destroy culture." (Caixa Catalunya, 2005)

Sustainable development is an issue gaining importance throughout the world and it has been declared one of the primary goals of the European Union. The concept of sustainability can to a certain degree and in appropriate ways be applied to all forms of tourism. As a baseline, the concept can be boiled down to economic, environmental and socio-cultural sustainability. Within the scope of sustainability, ecotourism and rural tourism emerge as tourism forms showing high compatibility. This publication is set in front of the background of sustainable tourism development and deals with the cultural and social impacts with the intention to put an emphasis on people instead of products and profits in order to make tourism more sustainable. The overall goal of "[…] development is to maximize the opportunities and minimize the adverse impacts […]" (Fennell, 2003, 14) on the local society and environment and at the same time to provide visitors and hosts with memorable experiences.

Social and cultural aspects are complex issues, characterised by their subjectivity, poor measurability and intangibility. Impacts only become evident in the long term, and remedial measures often can not compensate the damages already caused. Hence early planning, managerial action and continuous monitoring are crucial in order to ensure a sustainable social and cultural development.

Introduction

La Gomera was chosen to be presented as a case study. One of the main reasons for this choice is that La Gomera is comparable with many other European destinations effected by strong tourism development. Nevertheless its particularities have to be pointed out: the geographical location as a small neighbouring island of Tenerife, in a highly developed tourism environment, tourism is still in the early stages of development, rural tourism has a high potential for development. Due to the geographical isolation of the island, cultural and natural elements have been conserved in relatively pure and authentic forms.

The constant presence of tourists in a destination and in the every day lives of local residents, the tensions generated by the economic aspect of the activity, and the environmental degradation gradually give rise to increasing social pressure and cultural change.

The questions to be treated within the scope of this publication can be summarised as an analysis of means and ways to enhance positive and mitigate negative impacts of tourism on the local society and its cultural development.

1. Can intercultural exchange between tourists and the local population be influenced by managerial or legislative actions?
2. How can negative social impacts of tourism be mitigated?
3. By applying which managerial strategies can positive consequences of tourism be achieved for the cultural development of La Gomera?

The first part of this work will introduce theoretic concepts and present literature research regarding social and cultural impacts of tourism as well as quality management concepts and assessment, planning and monitoring tools to be integrated in a holistic management approach. The objective is to cover certain theories provided in literature and to create a framework for further implications.

The practical part of the publication presents the case study of La Gomera and intends to present the destination with regards to social and cultural characteristics linked to tourism development. The next step is the discussion and analysis of the social and cultural impacts of tourism on La Gomera and the application of selected theoretical concepts such as various indicators and SWOT analysis. Finally recommendations are presented in order to improve the social and cultural development with regards to tourism on La Gomera.

Methodology

The methodology chosen in order to obtain viable results and respond to the problem statements is a combination of literature research, statistical analysis and the integration of expert knowledge. For the theoretical part of the work, literature shall give knowledge about the existing concepts and theories regarding the topic. The statistical analysis is conducted by integrating secondary data from different official sources in a sustainability indicator set. The primary sources are the Statistical Institute of the Canary Islands (ISTAC), furthermore the Tourism Council of the Canary Islands and the association for rural tourism Ecotural Gomera.

The opinion of experts is obtained thanks to qualitative expert questionnaires conducted according to the *Delphi method* and integrated in the argumentation. The questionnaire "Encuesta Delphi sobre los aspectos sociales y culturales del turismo rural en La Gomera" was filled out by ten experts involved in the fields of tourism, culture and social affairs.

Delphi method

The research method is named after the oracle of Delphi which significantly influenced the history of the antique world from the VIII century b.c. until about 300 a.c. The modern method of expert questioning was firstly developed in the 1950s and applied in the fields of betting and military decisions.

Since then a myriad of definitions has been proposed and a series of applications and variations developed. The *Delphi questioning* as research procedure for specific circumstances is one of the preferred methods. It is used as an approach for problem solving and mainly for future prognostics. The technique represents a highly structured form of group communication process throughout which experts evaluate and give their opinions about situations or issues, "[...] when dealing with uncertainties in an area of imperfect knowledge". (Kaynak, 1994, in Häder, 2002, 21)

HÄDER defines different types of *Delphi questioning,* the one applied for this publication is the "questioning for the aggregation of ideas". (Häder, 2002, 30f) The objective of this approach is to obtain first suggestions and opinions about the current situation with regards to the problem to be dealt with. As a further step, the experts can be asked for possible solutions or suggestions for remedial actions. The questions are usually very concrete but should leave space for personal interpretation and the point of view of the expert. This approach is exclusively qualitative; on the contrary, other types of *Delphi questioning* include a first round of qualitative and following rounds of quantitative questions.

The main characteristics of Delphi questioning designed for the aggregation of ideas are: (Häder, 2002, 25-31)

- the use of standardised questionnaires,
- the questioning of an interdisciplinary group of experts within the respective field,
- the renunciation of statistical evaluation of the questionnaires,
- no claim to representation,
- relatively low number of experts (recommendation of six),
- qualitative summary of the arguments without anonymity.

2 CREATING A FRAMEWORK

Social and cultural aspects are not restricted to a specific type of tourism but concern tourism in general. This publication is embedded in the fields of ecotourism, rural tourism and sustainable tourism development as all three concepts consider social and cultural aspects in similar ways with a high degree of importance.

The first chapter will be dedicated to the creation of a general framework within which further arguments will be developed. As a first step ecotourism, rural tourism and sustainable development will be discussed not in order to create new definitions but in order to point out specific characteristics and common issues. In the second part the role of cultural and social aspects, often generalised and referred to as socio-cultural aspects, will be examined from different points of view.

2.1 An attempt to draw lines between the concepts of ecotourism, rural tourism and sustainable development

Throughout the last decades, characterised by emerging alternative tourism forms, the issues of ecotourism, rural tourism and sustainable tourism have been widely discussed on a global level. The existing attempts to define these concepts and to draw lines between them has not yet delivered satisfactory results.
It is a complex issue with blurred boundaries and limits between ecotourism, rural tourism and sustainable tourism products which leads to confusion among researchers, the industry and especially among tourists.
This situation is unclear due to the lack of internationally acknowledged definitions on one side and because the industry doesn't make much effort in order to change that on the other side, as profit can be made out of the situation. Hence all sorts of green-tourism products are offered under for example the label of "sustainable tourism" which do not fulfil the required characteristics. The inappropriate use of the term ecotourism for marketing reasons, the so called "green-washing", is used to make businesses appear sustainable. "Even so, there are many kinds of sustainable tourism that is not based on nature, and there is also nature tourism that is not sustainable." (TIES, 2003, 6) WIGHT (2001, in Weaver, 2001, 38) gives another example regarding this confusing situation: "even when

there is an educational focus, this may not necessarily relate to the environment" similarly; nature-based products are not necessarily ecotourism.

The inappropriate use of terms is a reason for misunderstandings; ecotourism and sustainable tourism are often deemed as synonyms. In certain fields and arguments they can be mutually exchanged but in general, the terms refer to completely different tourism concepts and therefore correct usage is essential. It is however, a field in which there is no way to draw a black and white picture.

2.1.1 Ecotourism

Surely the most commonly stated explanation of ecotourism in general literature is at the same time one of the earliest definitions, proposed by Ceballos-Lascurain in the 1980s. He defined ecotourism as: (Kaae, 2001, in Mc Cool, 2001, 33)

> travelling to relatively undisturbed or uncontaminated natural areas with the specific objective of studying, admiring, and enjoying the scenery and its wild plants and animals, as well as any existing cultural manifestations (both past and present) found in these areas.

This first attempt to define a concept which is seen as a form of tourism, philosophy, business, a marketing tool, a set of principals and values and a development program was followed by uncountable others which can all be broken down to three main components: "natural based, educational and sustainable management, which includes economic, social, cultural and ethical issues." (Diamantis, Westlake, 2001, in Font, Buckley, 2001, 33)

The International Ecotourism Society (TIES) defines ecotourism as "purposeful travel to natural areas to understand the culture and natural history of the environment, taking care not to alter the integrity of the ecosystem while producing economic opportunities that make the conservation of natural resources beneficial to local people." (Sirakaya, Jamal, Choi, in Weaver, 2001, 412)

Due to the multi-disciplinary concept, ecotourism requires "inter-sectoral alliances, comprehension and respect." (Planeta, 2005) It can not only be seen as a form of tourism but it's a social process which is difficult to be measured and regulated.

"Ecotourism markets are not homogenous groups." (Wight, 2001, in Weaver, 2001, 38) Therefore trade-off definitions of ecotourism are developed in order to cover the enormous range of ecotourism practice. The continuous scale ranges from "very weak" to "very strong" ecotourism. The nature-based component is the focal point of each definition. Educational and sustainability components don't even appear in the definition of very weak ecotourism, their emphasis becomes stronger going up the scale towards strong ecotourism. (Diamantis, Westlake, 2001, in Font, Buckley, 2001, 34)

Throughout the 1980s, when ecotourism first became popular, it was treated as the "panacea to all tourism-related problems in the destination areas" (Diamantis, Westlake, 2001, in Font, Buckley, 2001, 31), mainly in emerging countries. Ecotourism was seen as the universal remedy for the economic development of emerging countries. It was also thought as *the* concept to reverse negative impacts of mass tourism development in certain destinations. The views have changed since then and now the danger of over-reliance on ecotourism is postulated. Ecotourism can only be one of a series of tools for achieving sustainable development. (Halpenny, 2001, Weaver, 2001, 246)

According to different sources, motivations that differentiate ecotourists from mass tourists are: (Wight, 2001, in Weaver, 2001, 53)

- uncrowned locations,
- remote, wilderness areas,
- learning about natives and native cultures,
- community benefits,
- viewing plants and animals,
- physical challenges.

Another definition proposed by WIGHT (2001, in Weaver, 2001, 56) also referring to the difference in the attitude of tourists states that: "Ecotourists can be considered as a growing group of tourists who are shifting away from the consumption of *things*, towards the consumption of meaningful, learning and experiential vacations."

2.1.2 Sustainable Tourism Development

The baseline for sustainable development was published in the Brundtland Report, *Our Common Future* in which sustainable development is defined as one that "meets the needs of the present without comprising the ability of future generations to meet their own needs". (UNWCED 1987, in TIES, 2003, 4)

In other words the key elements of sustainability are: environmental conservation, social and cultural equity, profitable business and local benefits which sum up to the so called *triple-bottom-line*. (TIES, 2003, Planeta, 2005)

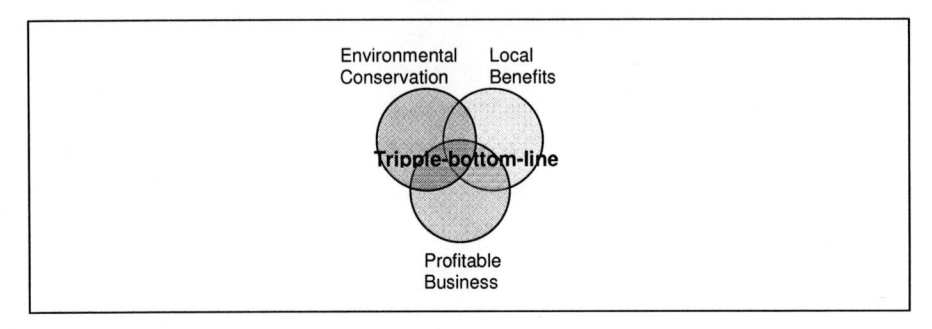

Figure 1: Visualisation of the Triple-bottom-line[1]

Sustainable tourism is therefore a tourism activity fulfilling the criteria of sustainability. "It aims to meet the needs of present tourists and host regions while protecting and enhancing environmental, social and economic values for the future." (Page, Dowling, 2002, 197) "It is envisaged as leading to management of all resources in such a way that economic, social, and aesthetic needs can be fulfilled while maintaining cultural integrity, essential ecological processes, biological diversity, and life support systems." (WTO, 1988, in TIES, 2003, 4) In other words, sustainable tourism should "[...] preserve the tourism's future seed corn". (Lane, 1994, in Font, Buckley, 2001, 29)

Among scientists, discussions have been going on, questioning if all types of tourism can become more sustainable or if certain types, such as coastal mass tourism, are not compatible with such principals. In general four points of view can be distinguished: "Polar opposites", where mass-tourism and sustainable tourism are absolute opposites. "A continuum", referring to different shades of sustainable and mass tourism finally meeting somewhere in the middle, "Movement", saying that mass tourism can move towards sustainability and finally "Convergence", stating that all types of tourism are compatible with the sustainability principles. (Swarbrooke, 2004, 9)

THE INTERNATIONAL ECOTOURISM SOCIETY (TIES, 2003, 4) is of the opinion that "the principles of sustainability can be applied to any type of tourism [...]" as well as to all sectors of the tourism industry. This point of view is also reflected in a statement of the WTO (2001, in TIES, 2003, 5) in which the differences of ecotourism and sustainable

---

[1] Planeta (2005)

tourism are discussed. Ecotourism is stated to be a segment within the tourism sector whereas "[...] sustainability principles should apply to all types of tourism activities, operations, establishments and projects, including conventional and alternative forms." Hence sustainable tourism is not a new form of tourism but can be a quality feature of all forms.

Of course some types of tourism are more compatible with the principles of sustainability, but that doesn't mean that any ecotourism venture is inherently more sustainable than other forms of tourism. The degree of sustainability depends on certain characteristics, such as the scale of the tourism industry, the impact on the physical environment, relations with the host community, socio-cultural impacts, economic impacts, the importance of the specific location, the quality of experience for the tourist and the tourists' behaviour. (Swarbrooke, 2004, 18)

The sustainable development principles are based on the triple-bottom-line concept and applicable to all types of business: (Page, Dowling, 2002, in Fennell, 2003, 13)

1. **Ecological sustainability**; development is compatible with the maintenance of essential ecological processes, biological diversity and biological resources.
2. **Social and cultural sustainability**; development increases people's control over their own lives, is compatible with the culture and values of people affected by it, and maintains and strengthens the community identity.
3. **Economic sustainability** fosters development that is economically efficient and resources are managed in a way that they will support future generations.

Certain critique is expressed regarding the current sustainable development approaches because of the strong emphasis on environmental factors. More and more companies are seeking to make their activities more sustainable but SWARBROOKE (2004, 6) states that neglecting economic and social dimensions "is a real problem in the debate of sustainability and sustainable tourism," as well as in practice. So far the industry has shown little interest in the social and cultural dimension of sustainability in terms of human resource management for example. (Swarbrooke, 2004, 10)

Sustainable development recognizes the need of balancing three basic goals: economic efficiency, social equity and environmental conservation. (Coccossis, 2004, in Coccossis, 2004, 7) There is not *one* absolute standard of sustainability but a wide spectrum of attitudes and commitment. The sustainable development spectrum reaches from a very weak until a very strong sustainability position depending on the considered characteristics and their emphasis. (Swarbrooke, 2004, 7)

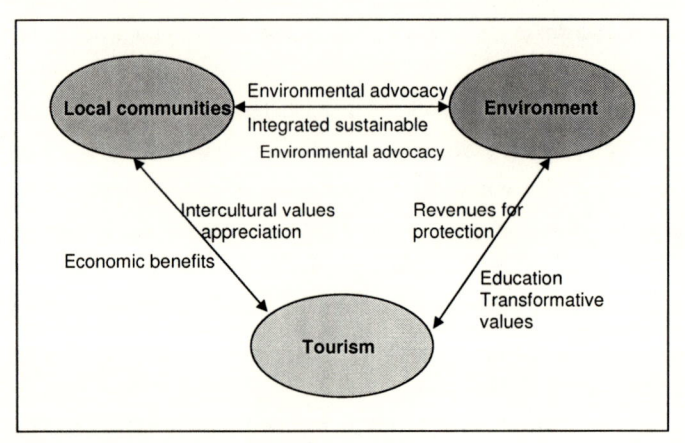

Figure 2: The sustainable tourism paradigm[2]

Whereas ecotourism has known a mainly industry driven development, sustainable tourism development is based on a strong European but also international initiative. International conferences, treaties and policies have marked the development of the sustainability concept. The Brundtland Report issued in 1987 can be considered as a starting point which was then reinforced in 1992 at the *Rio Summit* and the *Agenda 21*. The role of public bodies is important. Without regulations and policies the development of sustainability is deemed to fail in the framework of globalisation and capitalism.

2.1.3 Rural Tourism

Neither one general definition of rural tourism exists, nor one form of rural tourism. It is a type of tourism characterised by its widespread variety of offers and products. Bringing the concept to a baseline, one can consider rural tourism as a nature-based form of sustainable tourism taking place in rural areas and including physical activities and direct contact with the natural environment. The activities can vary from hiking, bike-rides, horseback riding and other sports to just contemplating the landscape and relaxing. The difference between ecotourism and rural tourism according to BROWN (ND) is the fact that latter is „[...] evocative of a broader spectrum of outdoor-based recreation, including

---

[2] Page, Dowling (2002), 227

hunting, fishing, camping and the use of recreational vehicles [...]" whereas ecotourism suggests active participation in the preservation of nature and a strong educational component.

As mentioned before rural tourism takes place in rustic areas which are, according to BUTLER (2001, in Weaver, 2001, 434) "[...] taken to be settled areas which are used primarily for agriculture, in which the pattern of settlement is permanent but may be either village based or dispersed." Hence rural tourism will not be located in a pristine nature but rather in a form of a human modified landscape.

A definition provided by FUENTES and TORRES (1994, in ACANTUR, 2005, 11) says rural tourism to be a tourism activity, practised in the countryside and made up by an offer of integrative leisure activities. One of the primary motivations of this form of tourism is contact with an authentic environment and interrelation with the local population. This definition brings the main characteristics to the point: active participation of the local population, complementary income, respect towards the natural and cultural heritage and personal contact of the tourists with the local population.

Rural tourism has changed throughout the years. It was once an activity focused on protected natural areas and national parks, now it is considered to have "a considerable potential for rural development". (Brown, ND) What had been expected from ecotourism for emerging countries is now expected from rural tourism development for economically disadvantaged rural areas. Tourism shall fill the gap that the decline of agriculture has created during the last decades. Many small scale farmers rely nowadays on additional income from tourism in order to reach an economical viability. Thanks to the economic benefits generated by rural tourism development, the rural exodus towards cities can be diminished, the population growth can be enhanced, labour created and the economy of the region diversified. It constitutes possible access for women to the labour market, stimulates the consumption of local products, preserves architectural heritage and maintains and enhances cultural development. (ACANTUR, 2005, 15f) Of course these benefits can easily turn into negative impacts if, for example, traditional activities are abandoned in favour of tourism. Hence the controlling and monitoring of an equilibrated, sustainable development are crucial.

The concept of sustainable development has been viewed as "an effective means of addressing the socio-economic challenges facing peripheral rural regions." (Sharpley, 2003, 38) "The use of rural-based tourism to help achieve the sustainability of the rural economies and societies, and compensate for the decline of traditional agriculture." (Swarbrooke, 2004, 11) Also, according to CABRINI (2002, 2) rural tourism can become a valuable contribution for rural economies and offer certain benefits: conservation and creation of labour, preservation of the landscape, conservation of services, protection of cultural heritage and support to the art and production of traditional craftwork. Hence tourism development can help to diversify the components of rural economies.

Especially in Europe, the development of rural tourism has been emphasised in areas where transformation of the rural sector has become important. But still the product range is rather limited. (Cabrini, 2002, 2) CABRINI (2002, 11) argues that in Europe the borders between ecotourism and rural tourism are rather blurred due to the intense and traditional interrelation between landscape, nature and human activity.

2.2 A common issue - cultural and social aspects

It is nowadays generally acknowledged that "all the stakeholders in tourism have both rights and responsibilities" (Hawkins, Lamoureux, 2001, in Weaver, 2001, 69) also in terms of social and cultural aspects. But still no profit generating issues are often neglected by the industry. Nevertheless this publication has a certain legitimacy, as social and cultural aspects have gained more and more importance throughout the last decades and will continue to do so in future. As lined out in the previous sections, social and cultural issues are integrative parts of ecotourism, rural tourism and sustainable tourism.

Within ecotourism principles, several points refer to social and cultural aspects: (Sirakaya, Jamal, Choi, 2001, in Weaver, 2001, 419-421)

- minimal negative impacts on the host environment,
- creation of necessary funds to promote sustained protection of ecological and socio-cultural resources,
- enhancement of interaction and understanding between visitors and hosts,
- contribution to the economic and social well-being of the local people.

MCINTYRE (1993, in Sirakaya, Jamal, Choi, 2001, in Weaver, 2001, 421) expressed this even more explicitly, saying that "the goal of ecotourism should be to improve the quality of life for both host and guest, provide quality experience for the visitors, and protect the natural and human environment including cultural, social and political dimensions."

"The term rural tourism is applied when the rural culture is a key component of the offered product." (Cabrini, 2002, 1) Other characteristics of rural tourism products are the personalised contact between hosts and guests, the opportunity to experience the physical and cultural environment of rural areas and as far as possible, the integration of visitors in traditional activities and the lifestyle of the rural population.

The social and cultural impacts of tourism are main aspects of the sustainable principles. The triple-bottom-line which builds the basic concept of sustainability, presents social equity and cultural sustainability besides economic and ecological sustainability as two of the key elements.

A number of scientists has been working on appropriate definitions and explaining the differences between ecotourism and rural tourism for more than a decade. Both, ecotourism and rural tourism are based on the concept of sustainability which integrates social and cultural issues as one of the three pillars of the concept.

3 SOCIAL AND CULTURAL ASPECTS OF TOURISM

According to a general definition often cited in literature, the social and cultural impacts of tourism are the way in which tourism is contributing to changes in the value system, individual behaviour, family relationships, collective lifestyle, safety levels, moral conduct, creative expressions, traditional ceremonies and community structure. (Page, Dowling, 2002, 170) An important characteristic of social and cultural impacts is the fact that they are intangible, hybrid and less perceivable than ecologic and economic factors. Therefore it is a big challenge to identify and measure social and cultural effects.

As illustrated in figure 3, tourism impacts are often considered as a triangle shaped model, with an economic, an environmental and a social and cultural impact area. Nevertheless impacts can not always be attributed to one specific domain but rather have overlapping, multidimensional characteristics. MATHIESON and WALL (1982, in Boyne, 2003, in Hall, 2003, 23) propose the term "cross impacts" in order to explain the existence of interplays of economic, environmental and socio-cultural effects.

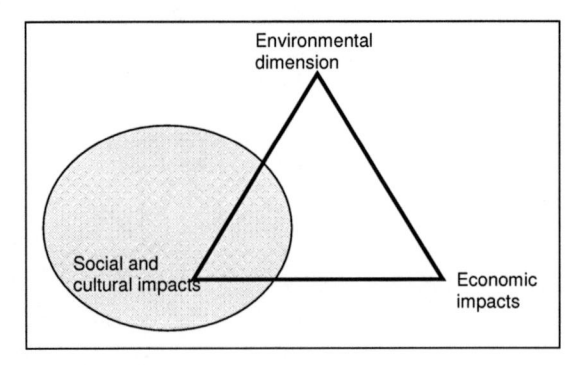

Figure 3: Tourism impact model[3]

BRUNT and COURTNEY (1999, in Boyne, 2003, in Hall, 2003, 25) define three sub-groups of social and cultural impacts. Firstly, they mention general social impacts, due to general tourism development, for example infrastructure and creation of employment. Secondly, effects on the host society are identified that occur at the moment of interaction with

---

[3] after Butler (1974), in Hall (2003), 22

tourists, phenomena such as *acculturation*. As a third group, cultural impacts are defined. Whereas the general social impacts might occur in the short term, changes of social conduct and cultural impacts only become evident in the long run.

When conducting research on social and cultural impacts of tourism, three aspects have to be taken into consideration: the host culture, the tourist and the relationship between tourist and host. (Page, Dowling, 2002, 170) Thus one has to examine the local population and its attitude towards tourism, the tourists and their expectations and attitude towards the host culture and finally their interaction, the form of contact and the modalities of interaction. As stated in literature, the impacts will be greatest when there is a large contrast between the culture of the receiving society and the culture of origin. (Burns, Holden, 1995, in Manson, 2003, 43)

As social and cultural impacts are often very difficult to be distinguished, in literature they are mostly referred to as socio-cultural effects. Even though a separation is necessary, at this stage a general overview of the socio-cultural impacts as stated by FINGUEROLA (in Wearing, 2001, in Weaver, 2001, 397) should classify the effects and introduce into the topic.

1. Impacts on population structure
    a. Size of population
    b. Age/sex composition
    c. Modification of family size
    d. Rural-urban transformation of population

2. Transformation of types of occupation
    a. Impact on /of language and qualification
    b. Impact on occupation distribution by sector
    c. Demand for female labour
    d. Increase in seasonality of employment

3. Transformation of values
    a. Political
    b. Social
    c. Religious
    d. Moral

4. Influence on traditional way of life
   a. Art, music and folklore
   b. Habits and customs
   c. Daily living

5. Modification of consumption patterns
   a. Qualitative alterations
   b. Quantitative alterations

3.1 Culture and cultural aspects of tourism

In order to discuss social and cultural aspects of tourism, a clear definition of culture has to be agreed on beforehand. The study of culture lies in the field of anthropology and theories date back to antique Greek times. Throughout the centuries a flood of definitions and theories has been proposed. BODLEY, suggests culture to be "the patterns of behaviour and thinking that people living in social groups learn, create and share." (Bodley, 1997) This very general definition covers the entire range of aspects of the concept of culture. "A people's culture includes their beliefs, rules of behaviour, language, rituals, art, technology, clothing, ways of producing and cooking food, religion and political and economic systems." (Bodley, 1997) Whereas anthropologists intend to create an exhaustive list of all contents of culture, not even an open-ended list would be appropriate in order to state all aspects of culture as it is a constantly changing concept. To put it in a nutshell, one can see culture as the way of life shared by a specific group of people.

As already mentioned in the definition, culture has certain very specific characteristics. (Bodley, 1997) Culture is based on symbols which are understood among people from the same society and communicates certain ideas, feelings and attitudes.
Differently to what early theories stated, culture is not inherited but learned and taught. The process transmitting cultural values and behaviours to members of the society is referred to as *enculturation*. The process starts right after birth and continues throughout the entire lifetime. Another important component of culture is its constant state of change caused by internal and external influences.
Culture is a system of common ways of thinking and behaviours shared by the members of one group or society. The fact that culture adapts to changes in the world surrounding the

society has ensured the survival of human beings. It is a flexible and adjustable system, very responsive to any changes of the environment and thus influences the life of people. (Bodley, 1997)

In order to concretise the concept of culture, three categories are defined. "Material culture" includes all products manufactured by the society, modalities of how food and other goods are produced, the forms of exchange as well as the technologies and techniques used. "Social culture" refers to the social structure and organisation of a group of people, kinship and family relations, work life, leadership and political power. The third category is the "ideological culture" which includes all forms of beliefs, value systems and religions. In anthropological literature a fourth category has been added: "art". It can be considered as the combination of material and ideological culture and has a special position being disconnected from basic human needs being located on top of the MASLOWS' pyramid of needs it satisfies the human need of self-expression.

Cultural exchange in tourism

Culture can be categorised in "material culture", "social culture" and "ideological culture". Furthermore a distinction between conscious and subconscious contents is made in literature.

The question regarding the level on which intercultural exchange exists and which parts are most affected by external influences, has to be discussed. As shown in the following figure, the host culture is a concept that has three levels. The central part refers to the "ideological culture", to the value systems of a society, ideologies, religions and beliefs. This part of a society's culture is the most private and the last to be effected by changes and influences. It is developed and transmitted over generations and forms an important part of the cultural identity. Changes on this level only occur on the long term.

The second level is the "behavioural culture" which means the attitude and behaviour of the host culture in their private lives and interaction with others. It includes factors such as social relations, language, work relationships and can be identified as the category of social culture.

The outer level shows the so called "material culture". It refers to all elements commercialized and explicitly offered to the tourist in form of products and performance. It is the external level and refers to the "visible part" of culture, like the tip of an iceberg. The exchange occurring on this level is based on economics. Changes and adaptation processes are most frequent on the outer level, as local people are willing to modify their offers in order to satisfy the tourists' needs.

Changes in behaviour, language and other issues of "behavioural culture" occur less easily and changes require more time. A continuous and ongoing process of intercultural exchange and external influences is necessary to penetrate the behavioural system of a society and cause changes.

Modifications on the "ideological level" only occur over long periods. Constant and long lasting influences of tourism "[...] lead to a longer-term, gradual change in a society's values, beliefs, and cultural practices". (Boyne, 2003, in Hall, 2003, 25)

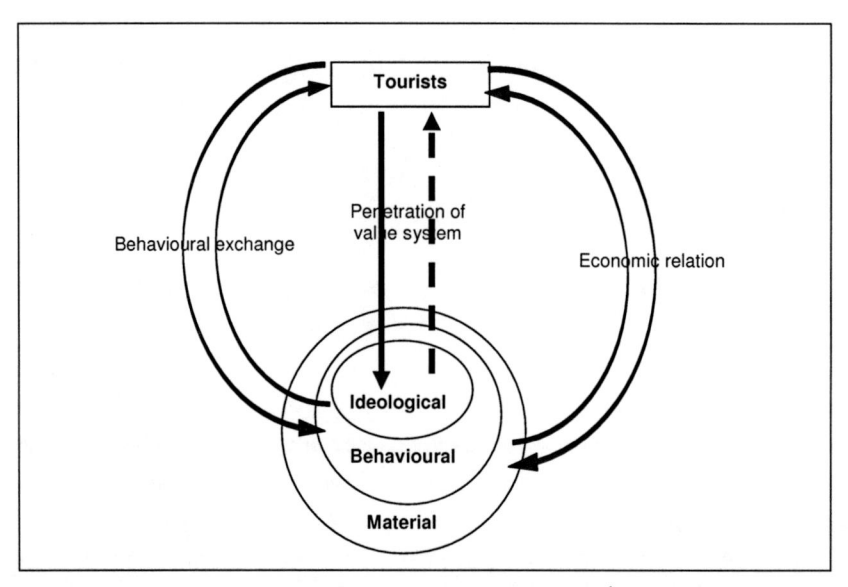

Figure 4: Intercultural exchange between host culture and tourists[4]

Researchers in the field of tourism and anthropology claim that cultural exchange during holidays takes place on at least three levels: the culture of the visitor, of the host society and a third level which is referred to as "tourist culture". It defines an artificial culture that only exists temporarily when people are on holidays, travelling in foreign countries and playing the role of a tourist. The tourist culture is similar for all tourists independent of their nationality. (Binder, 2002, 17-18)

---

[4] elaboration by the author

Tourism is based on interpersonal contact and relationships, and can therefore be considered as a two-way interactive process of cultural exchange between the host and the visitor. Both sides have to be considered when analysing cultural aspects or impacts of tourism. In many cases, tourism is an unbalanced process of intercultural exchange. In general, the more severe the socio-cultural impacts, the greater the cultural difference between the host and the visitor. On the other hand, the bigger the contrast between the two cultures, the more exotic or special the host culture is perceived to be by the tourist, so the potential of cultural attraction is greater. The following elements decide the cultural attractiveness of a destination: (Ritchie, Zins, 1978, in Manson, 2003, 43)

- craftwork
- language
- traditions, legends and rites
- gastronomy
- art and music
- history of the area, including visual artefacts
- types of work of the local population
- architecture
- religion, including the experiences of manifestations
- educational system
- clothing and typical dresses
- leisure activities

Certain types of tourists such as cultural tourists, ethnic tourists, rural tourists and ecotourists are more specifically seeking an inspiring cultural experience during their holidays. One can argue that these forms of tourism usually don't attract the masses and therefore create less effects even though this tourism is usually more involved in the cultural life of the destination.

Cultural Impacts of tourism

Cultural impacts refer to actions that lead to the transformation of lifestyle and cultural manifestations; any change of social norms, values, beliefs, traditional products and lifestyle, anything that gradually affects interpersonal and inter-communitarian relations. (Izquierdo, Salas, 1999, 39)

Within the field of tourism research, two opposite points of view have come up and been discussed. At the beginning, tourism was celebrated as a "vehicle for world peace" that was said to be capable of generating cultural harmony among people. Since then that opinion has changed radically; tourism is now considered as an "agent of cultural conflict". (Robinson, 1999, in Robinson, Boniface, 1999, 6) Today the situation has to be seen to be even more distinctive. Tourism can have positive influences on a destination's culture and on mutual understanding, but it can equally be the cause for destruction and harm of cultural development.

Hence positive and negative impacts on the host population might occur; in literature they are often referred to as "social costs and benefits of tourism".

Cultural Impacts of Tourism	
Benefits	**Costs**
• Stimulation of the interest of the administration and the local population towards historic and ethnographical heritage • Rebirth of local art, crafts and traditional cultural activities • Renewal of local architectural tradition • Rehabilitation and preservation of existing architecture • Reinforcement of the cultural identity and pride of the population • Tourism investments support cultural activities • Promotion of the need to conserve areas of outstanding cultural value • Promotion of the culture in foreign countries can lead to more understanding, respect and enhance communication • Positive cultural changes, referring to tolerance and openness	• The commercialisation of culture and local products • Violation of holy celebrations and places • Manipulation and exfoliation of historic and ethnographical heritage • Changes in traditional architecture • Degradation and loss of certain traditions • Loss of cultural identity and authenticity • Reproduction of handicrafts as souvenirs; theft of cultural property such as songs, arts • Erosion of cultural values with the introduction of the tourist values

Figure 5: Positive and negative social impacts of tourism[5]

---

[5] after Izquierdo, Salas (1999), Boyne (2003), in Hall (2003)

The listing of both, negative and positive impacts shown in the figure below must neither be considered to be exhaustive nor compelling. These are effects that might occur in tourist destinations depending on a series of external and internal factors.

Some of the aspects, such as cultural identity, are mentioned on the cost and benefit side. This is due to the ambiguous effects that might occur. Depending on the specific situation, tourism can either enhance the cultural identity among the locals by esteeming and promoting local culture outside the destination and also among the local population or, on the contrary, if it commercialises and adapts cultural aspects the local population looses identification with its culture.

Culture is an abstract concept which underlies a continuous, natural process of change and evolution. The challenge for tourism and cultural planners is to ensure that tourism promotes the conservation of the local culture without hindering its' natural modifications (Schyvens, 1999, in Page, Dowling, 177). It would be fatal to stop the natural development process due to tourism interests; an artificial culture, a kind of role play would be the result. On the other hand, accelerated and forced cultural changes due to tourism might also harm the local community.

Commercialisation of culture

In today's world, the market decides upon the price of goods and services. Also cultural themes and traditional arts become tradable goods on the global tourism market.

Those sellable elements of the local culture are the first to be modified according to the needs and demands of the market. Traditional rites, dances, songs and events are put on stage and promoted like a theatre play. The question, where lived culture ends and souvenir kitsch starts is not easy to be answered. The same happens with tangible goods, most souvenirs that are sold in tourism destinations are mass production, don't have anything to do with traditional production methods and imitate local craftwork. Often local art objects are reproduced in simplified forms, in cheap mass production in foreign countries and then sold to tourists.

So called 'culture brokers' act as middlemen between the tourists and the local population in order to plan and promote cultural items. These culture brokers are often foreigners that don't even know the culture they are intending to sell and cultural resources are selected and valued according to market analysis and market values. (Binder, 2002, 22)

The commercialisation of culture can lead to changes in the meaning and importance of cultural acts for the local population. Traditional events turn into tourist events where local people are paid to perform like actors. As a consequence the traditional meaning of the event gets lost and it becomes a commercialised show.

There are many examples all over the world showing the same development, such as traditional dancing in New Zealand and Hawaii. According to MANSON (2003, 46) those so called pseudo-events share a series of characteristics: they are planned and not spontaneous, they are performed on demand, on dates that satisfy the tourism industry, and they loose the relationship to the traditional elements on which they are based. An important aspect that is mentioned by WILLIAM (in Manson, 2003, 46) is the fact that pseudo-events eventually become the real event that replaces the traditional and authentic one.

Demonstration effect

As mentioned earlier, differences can be observed between the every day culture of the tourists and so called "tourist culture". A change of behavioural patterns occurs when people leave their habitual surroundings to go on holiday. Those changes become evident through the generous spending behaviour of tourists, loosened moral understanding, laziness and relaxed and passive behaviour. (Binder, 2002, 19) Hence local people get to know this side of tourism which may lead to a misinterpretation of the actual standards and culture in the countries of origin. This demonstration of the differences may lead to a process of self reflection of the local population about their financial situation, their standard of living etc.

Imitation effect

Imitation is a consequence of cultural differences that become evident when tourists and hosts come together. PRATT (1992, cited in Howforth, Munt, 1998, 244) calls this process "transculturation" and describes it as the way in which marginalised or subordinated groups select and adapt materials transmitted to them by dominant "metropolitan cultures". Researchers speak of an imitation effect when the local population intends to imitate and adapt the lifestyle of tourists. This happens when tourism creates new demands and needs in a destination. In general young people are more sensitive to external influences and are more willing to adapt and change. The degree of adaptation and imitation highly depends on the level of cultural contrast between the host and local culture. In the end, the imitation of foreign behaviour and adaptation of other ways of life can cause a feeling of uprooting among the local population.

Acculturation

Due to continuous cultural influence from outside and import of foreign cultural elements, a process of cultural change is initiated at the destination. The process of *acculturation* can also be seen as the changes that occur in a culture when different groups of people come together. LEA (1988, in Wearing, 2001, in Weaver, 2001, 404) defines the phenomenon of *acculturation* as the process whereby people borrow from each other's cultural heritage. One has to take in mind that the cultural exchange based on tourism in many cases comprises a dominating and a dominated culture, hence the process of *acculturation* often is asymmetric, unnatural and accelerated and can therefore lead to problems.

Acculturation symbolizes the relationship of power between the tourist and host as the local population, in most cases, tries to adapt to the needs and demands of tourists. HOWFORTH and MUNT (1998, 244) argue that tourism inevitably creates the effect of adaptation and therefore prohibits any authentic experience. No local society in constant contact with tourism can resist cultural changes, so it therefore demonstrates modified cultural traits.

Throughout the last decades, the understanding of cultural exchange between hosts and tourists has changed substantially. In the early 1960s tourism was understood to have potentially positive impacts and to promote and enhance global understanding; the opinions of researchers have changed completely since then. KRIPPENDORF (1987, in Manson, 2003, 45) noted that travelling to countries presenting big cultural differences does not diminish prejudice, but rather intensifies it. Hence tourism does not resolve misunderstandings but rather reinforces cultural stereotypes.

3.2 Society and social aspects

The term society refers to a structured group of people with certain common characteristics, such as living environment, institutions, culture and interaction with each other. As members of a society, people acquire knowledge, beliefs, art, moral laws, customs and other capabilities and customs that are inherent characteristics of the specific group.

Social aspects, as already discussed previously, are constantly exposed to a multitude of external influences and changes. It is therefore very difficult to filter and distinguish modifications caused by tourism. The following social aspects are above all affected by tourism and have to be considered and analysed:

- Labour
- Education
- Social relations
- Standards of living
- Social structure
- Administrational structure
- Migration flows
- Geographical impacts

Social impacts of tourism

A general definition says that social impacts are the changes in social structures and relations due to the development of tourism in a destination. (Izquierdo, Salas, 1999, 39) According to PRASAD, (1987, in Wearing, 2001, in Weaver, 2001, 397) social impacts are influences that come to bear upon the host society as a result of tourist contact. They can hence be defined as the direct and indirect results of interpersonal relations that occur between the local residents and visitors during the holidays of the latter.

Besides changes in the host culture, tourism also shows severe influences on the social structure of the local society; for example on employment. At first sight, tourism is an employment creator but in numerous cases, the creation of jobs in the field of tourism causes the loss of workplaces in other industries. Traditional industries, such as farming and craftwork, are particularly sensitive to this type of change. The first sector in which new jobs are available is the construction industry. As a consequence, due to the availability of jobs people might move away from their area of origin and cause a rural exodus which leaves rural areas deserted. On the other side tourism development is always accompanied by an urbanisation process in originally low populated zones where new infrastructure and facilities for tourism are created. (Binder, 2002, 22)

Alternative forms of tourism tend to invert the mentioned negative employment effects by augmenting the demand for local products and therefore enhancing the job perspectives in traditional industries. Besides this, sustainable tourism creates long-term employment particularly open to local people who can benefit from their knowledge of the zone. Citing CEBALLOS-LASCURÁIN (1992, in Wearing, 2001, in Weaver, 2001, 402) local people possess the practical and ancestral knowledge of the natural features of the area.

Nevertheless it is often the case that tourism (and also ecotourism) ventures are owned by expatriates and foreigners. Foreign involvement can cause enormous financial effects, an economic leakage, when tourism incomes are not reinvested in the destination but rather in foreign countries.

Another important social issue is the influence of tourism on the traditional gender roles. The tourism industry creates jobs and working possibilities to a big extent for women. Widening the opportunities for women often reduces their dependence and may affect family relationships especially in developing areas. (Wearing, 2001, in Weaver, 2001, 401f) Tourism is creator of a multitude of social costs and benefits in a destination, the challenge is to ensure a balanced development for the local population.

The following listing of social impacts is not exhaustive and the single effects might or might not occur, depending on a series of internal and external factors.

Social Impacts of Tourism

Benefits

- Creation of employment that requires a low level of specialisation
- Revitalization of poor and non-industrial regions due to the increase in demand for accommodating and additional services
- Revival of the social and cultural life of the local population
- Increase in the income level in a region, which leads to a higher standard of living for the local population
- The improved infrastructure in tourism destination influences the standard of living in a positive way
- Some researchers state more intercultural understanding and intercultural exchange as a social benefit. This fact can easily shift to the opposite side.
- Increase in the market for local products, sustaining traditional customs and practices (depending on form of tourism)
- Greater opportunities for financial freedom for women

Costs

- The terziarisation leads to a decline of traditional activities. (farming)
- Co-existence with tourism is difficult
- Increase in land prices and speculation.
- Massification and overcrowded destinations lead to stress for hosts and tourists
- Many families depend economically on tourism which is very sensitive to the surrounding economic situation
- Changes in social life due to working hours in the tourism industry
- Increased wealth generated by tourism can unbalance traditional social structures
- Tourism businesses attract foreign workforces which often occupy the highest positions
- Crime rate and adoption of illegal economies
- Undermining of family structures
- Tensions within a community between those for and against tourism.
- Increased costs of living in tourism destinations

Figure 6: Positive and negative social impacts of tourism[6]

---

[6] after Wearing (2001), in Weaver (2001), Binder (2002)

3.3 Factors influencing the social and cultural impacts

Social and cultural impacts are not independent concepts but on the contrary they are influenced by a series of factors which can either reinforce or moderate negative impacts. Factors such as the number and nationality of the tourists, the duration of the stay and the type of tourism attracted play an important role when it comes to of social and cultural impacts. PRATT (in Howforth, Munt, 1998, 243) refers to "contact zones", "social spaces" where disparate cultures meet, clash, grapple with each other, often in highly asymmetrical relations of domination and subordination. The scale can reach from feelings of cultural loss and estrangement, which leads to rejection of tourism development to a revitalization of cultural heritage.

By managing these factors, the impacts of tourism can either be avoided or mitigated. Bad management, on the other hand, can aggravate the negative impacts. It is the objective of this publication to analyse how and by applying which concepts, impacts can be influenced in a favourable way.

Seasonality can reinforce negative impacts of tourism as the local population is forced to change its way of life during several months, depending on the tourism seasons. (Manson, 2003, 44) This fact nourishes the reluctance of the host population towards tourism as it creates economical benefits only during a certain period and forces people to find other activities to do during low seasons. Seasonality leads to an overload of work, overcrowded destinations and stress during the high season and deserted tourist resorts, empty accommodation facilities and little employment during the rest of the year.

Impacts, and their degree, also vary according to the type of tourism found in a destination. Sustainable tourism of course will cause more benefits regarding a society's culture, whereas mass tourism and conventional forms of tourism are accompanied by mainly negative impacts on the host culture. Certain scientists argue that the peril of ecotourism compared to mass tourism is perhaps greater as ecotourists travel to very sensitive destinations in order to learn about their cultures and societies. The level of interaction with the host community is therefore very elevated. (Halpenny, 2001, in Weaver, 2001, 245) This relation between the type of tourism and impact depends on the specific characteristics of the different tourism forms, such as the form of travel, key elements, number of tourists and special interests.

SMITH (1989, in Page, Dowling, 2002, 171) defines seven types of tourists which are characterised by a specific degree of adaptation to local norms. Besides, the model also states the number of tourists that is typical for each type of tourism. These two factors are directly linked with the level of social and cultural impacts on the local community.

Type of tourist	Numbers of tourists	Adaptation to local norms
Explorer	Very limited	Accepts fully
Elite	Rarely seen	Adapts fully
Off-beat	Uncommon but seen	Adapts well
Unusual	Occasional	Adapts somewhat
Incipient mass	Steady flow	Seeks Western amenities
Mass	Continuous flow	Expects Western amenities
Charter	Massive arrivals	Demands Western amenities

Table 1: Types of tourists and their adaptation to local norms[7]

As presented in this table, only tourism occurring on a non-regular basis and with limited numbers allows tourists to accept and adapt to local norms and customs. With increasing numbers of tourists and steady flows of visitors in a destination, the expectations and demands for special tourist amenities and services strengthen and tourists are not willing to adapt to local customs anymore. They are neither looking for direct contact with the host culture anymore, nor getting to know a different way of life, but want to enjoy their own lifestyle and amenities with a high level of quality.

As stated in literature, the duration of the stay plays an important role when it comes to determine the degree of social and cultural impacts. Researchers argue that the shorter an intercultural exchange lasts, the more superficial and short-lasting are the eventual impacts. There is no time for an in-depth cultural exchange which might cause effects such as *acculturation* and imitation.

In countries with strong religious codes, altered social values presented by tourists will be rejected and can lead to a situation of tension between the tourists and the host population. Within the bounds of this issue, the degree of strength and coherence of the local society and culture also enters. (Swarbrooke, 2004, 71)

The degree of contrast between the local culture of the host region and the visitors' culture profoundly influences the weight of negative impacts. The bigger the cultural difference, the more severe the impacts might be on the host culture. Said differently, the level of

---

[7] Smith (1989), in Page, Dowling (2002), 171

economic and social development of the local community has a determining role. (Swarbrooke, 2004, 71)

3.4 Difficulties to measure social and cultural impacts

According to CARTER (1987, in Wearing, 2001, in Weaver 2001, 398), the dynamic state of culture makes changes inevitable, even essential. However, tourism can accelerate and manipulate these changes in the host culture.

The characteristic of continuous cultural evolution complicates the determination and assessment of impacts as it occurs constantly, is due to different reasons and is under various influences. It is therefore hardly possible to determine the reasons for a change as it is, for the most part, an interplay of various factors such as globalisation, migration and the general economic situation. The isolation of the precise causes or processes leading to specific impacts is next to impossible: is tourism the principal agent of change or is it part of a wider process of development in a particular destination? (Page, Dowling, 2002, 149)
Another aspect disfavouring the research of social and cultural impacts of tourism is the reluctant position and disinterest of tourism agencies and companies involved in the industry. The open marketplace does not require the use of social and environmental impact monitoring tools and, at present, hardly any agents provide assistance and funding for research or the development of monitoring mechanisms. (TIES, 2005)

Conclusion

Social and cultural impacts of tourism are, in comparison with economic and ecological impacts, the least measurable and less evident consequences of tourism. Often social changes occur and no specific reason can be identified. Social and cultural development is influenced by a series of factors, of which tourism is just one. Social and cultural impacts are hardly measurable but underlie the more subjective evaluation methods, taking into account the opinions and perceptions of people. For the industry, these aspects are less important than economic factors but one has to consider the high importance social and cultural issues have for people. Culture transmits values and gives directions in life and a balanced society should provide a certain backing for its members. Culture and society create an essential framework for people to live together. Negative influences can destroy the balance of this sensitive structure and delicate equilibrium. Research and awareness of these concepts are important in order to ensure a sustainable development of tourism.

4 QUALITY MANAGEMENT IN TOURISM

Tourism has become one of the major industries, characterised by an enormous variety of tourism products and tourists becoming more and more experienced and demanding. With the arrival of multinational businesses involved in tourism, global hotel chains and "[...] giant tourism operations with activities that stretch from one end of the globe to the other, the need to offer guaranteed quality with products that have been standardised almost to an industrial level has become inescapable." (Keller, 1997, in Keller, 1997, 7)

This chapter deals with the broad issue of quality management in tourism. It should provide a theoretical overview of current discussion in literature as well as established models and theories. As an introduction, the concept of quality is discussed from different points of view and taking into account various approaches, aspects and theories with a focus on the social dimension of quality. As a second part, the question of quality measurement will be dealt with and the most common models of quality assessment are presented. The last part is dedicated to the management of quality not on a business level but on the more ample destination level. Two similar approaches will be presented, *Total Quality Management* (TQM) and *Integrated Quality Management* (IQM).

4.1 Concept of Quality

POMPL (1997, in Pompl, Dreyer, 1997, 2) defines quality as a complex, multi-characteristic, bi-pole continuum, relative, multi-dimensional and dynamic concept. KELLER (1997, in Keller, 1997, 8) says quality to be an "al-embracing term". He states very clearly that the concept of quality can not be explained by providing an unequivocal definition. Due to the common usage of the term in different settings, circumstances and referring to different concepts makes further specifications necessary.

The sensation of good or bad quality derives from the perception of a series of attributes or characteristics making up a service. Its evaluation lies on a continuous scale between the extreme points *total satisfaction* and *total dissatisfaction*. Quality is subjective and relative, depending on the persons involved, other available alternatives and the specific situation. It consists of a certain number of dimensions: a content dimension and a performance and a time dimension. The dynamic characteristics of quality refer to the ever changing customer demands and the development of quality levels required. (Pompl, 1997, in Pompl, Dreyer, 1997, 2)

A proposal had been brought up saying that the meaning and understanding of the term "quality" varies among different cultures and nations. The assumption was confirmed by a study conducted by the Spanish Quality Association, presenting the different implications of quality in several European countries. (Brent, Crouch, 1997, in Keller, 1997, 132)

> The British see quality as value for money. Germans view quality in terms of security and guarantee of standards. The French associate the term quality with aesthetics and quality of life. To the Italians, quality is related to luxury and authenticity. The message: tourism operators must be able to deliver the appropriate quality message to the right audience.

In literature, requirements are distinguished, the total of all expectations sum up to the total quality perceived by the tourists. *Must-be requirements* are basic component that are absolutely required; their non-performance leads to an unsatisfactory total quality. On the other side, their fulfilment does not necessarily increase perceived quality. Such *must-be requirements* are often defined by law, can be developed as industry specific customs, or product specific requirements and can lead to official sanctions.

Should requirements refer to elements which are desired but do not decide upon total performance failure. However their existence or non-existence does influence the overall satisfaction of tourists in a positive and respectively negative way, proportional to the degree of fulfilment.

Can requirements, also called *added-values*, have the greatest influence upon customer satisfaction. Those features are neither explicitly expressed nor expected. Therefore the performance of so called "extras" influences the overall satisfaction in a positive way. (Pompl, 1997, in Pompl, Dreyer, 1997, 27) Quality in tourism is created by value-added features rather than the core features of a service. (Freyer, 1997, in Keller, 1997, 251)

Besides their importance, features can also be distinguished according to their objective or subjective perception. *Scaleable requirements* refer to measurable components such as the room size or attractions provided for tourists. Due to their objective and easily expressible characteristics, these aspects are often used for promotional purposes. *Attractive requirements* are more subjective factors that become apparent throughout the stay and are not always expected; therefore they have the greatest influence on the ultimate quality level of the experience. (European Commission, 1999, 12)

Interpersonal relations have a special importance when it comes to the perception of quality. Contact might occur on different levels: firstly the contact between service providers or local people and tourists, and secondly the relations among tourists themselves. The former is often referred to as *Hospitality management* which according to KELLER (1997, in Keller, 1997, 10) is defined as "[...] ensuring that relations between host and guest are warm and amicable [...]" and can not be left to chance. The latter refers to the so called *interaction potential* which has a great influence on the overall quality perception. It includes all possible contacts and interactions among tourists during the vacation period. (Pompl, 1997, in Pompl, Dreyer, 1997, 17) Contacts can have positive effects by stimulating the holiday experience but can also result in very negative feelings. The interest of tourists in socialising depends on their expectations, personality, character and the type of holiday.

KELLER (1997, in Keller, 1997, 10) distinguishes another quality dimension, the *quality of experience* which refers to the "[...] appropriate atmosphere of hospitality [...]" hence in encompasses the quality of personal contacts. Not only the contact between tourist and service provider is important, but the tourist himself plays a major role in the creation of his own experiences and for those of other tourists consuming the service at the same time.

In HAYWOOD-FARMERS' *Model of service quality,* the interaction between customer and service provider plays a very important role. First of all he classifies service entities according to their "degree of customisation, degree of contact and interaction and degree of labour intensity". (Hope, 1997, in Keller, 1997, 60f) According to HAYWOOD-FARMER the service quality can be boiled down to a triangular model, based on the "[...] systems for delivery (physical process), [...]" the interaction between customer and provider during the production process and the "[...] discretion or judgement required to customise the service (professional judgement)". (Hope, 1997, in Keller, 1997, 60) A significant fact is that the three facets of service quality have to be balanced appropriately. In other words, a quasi-manufacturing service provider should emphasize the physical process, whereas contact intensive services should enhance the professional judgement and behaviour of their employees.

Customer satisfaction is often used in order to evaluate the quality of a service, but it can not be considered to be a valid indicator since important aspects, such as environmental and social quality, are completely neglected. As mentioned earlier, quality evaluation always refers to a subjective measurement. It is based on a complex psychological comparison between expected and perceived performance. (Pompl, 1997, in Pompl, Dreyer, 1997, 8) The former is influenced by the promises communicated through the offer, personal experiences and quality-prices relationship. The latter refers to the quality performed as perceived by the customer. This relationship can be expressed by the following formula. (Langer, 1997, 77) The first formula refers to the pure difference between perception and expectation, whereas the second takes the actual importance of the specific components into account.

> *Service Quality = Perception – Expectations*
> *Service Quality = Importance * (Perception – Expectations)*

The evaluation of service quality is a complex task and objectivity is hardly achievable. Heterogeneity of the service performance is due to these factors: human beings and the specific situation. Furthermore, tourism services do include a series of services which are provided at the same time or in consequence by different service providers. Therefore they are often referred to as "collective services". (Pompl, 1997, in Pomple, Dreyer, 1997, 7) This specific characteristic of tourism makes quality management even more difficult as no single service provider can guarantee the quality level of the whole tourism product. KELLER (1997, in Keller, 1997, 12) postulates the inherent need for cooperation between individual producers of tourism services on the destination level.

4.2 Measurement of Quality

"Service Quality measurement is difficult because of the complex nature of interrelated service bundles [...] and because of the subjective nature of the quality assessments through customers." (Weiermair, 1997, in Keller, 1997, 44) Quality that can not be measured is unsuitable as a planning- management- and controlling tool. (Scharitzer, 1997, in Pompl, Dreyer, 1997, 56) One of the most important issues is therefore the definition of evaluation and measurement criteria.

In literature, two types of assessment methods are distinguished on quality measurement: the *incident-based* models and the *attribute-based* methods. The former describe and evaluate the consequences of customer experiences, positive or negative. The latter measures service quality perception according to specific attribute lists. (Langer, 1997, 73) Different points of view and opinions always exist when it comes to the evaluation of quality. When talking about the evaluation of interpersonal contacts and the quality of tourist-host relationships, it is clear that two sides exist which both have very subjective opinions based on perception. Quality of services always also depends on a framework and on the situation; the persons involved (service provider and external factor), the environment, materials used, the production processes and organisation. (Scharitzer, 1997, in Pompl, Dreyer, 1997, 60)

In order to obtain the required information, different techniques can be applied. *Observation* is defined as a target oriented and systemised recording of circumstances and behaviour or conduct by a third person who is not involved in the situation. (Scharitzer, 1997, in Pompl, Dreyer, 1997, 67-69) A second and broader method which could be used is surveys. The two main types are the *complaint analysis* and the *FRAP-analysis*. The first refers to the detailed analysis of complaints by conducting interviews with the concerned customers. The *frequency-relevance analysis of problems* (FRAP) considers the importance of problems and the frequency with which they occur. (Scharitzer, 1997, in Pompl, Dreyer, 1997, 69-74) A qualitative approach of specific interest is the method of *story telling*. It can provide detailed information about critical situations by surveying the consumer with open questions and open ended interviews. (Weiermair, 1997, in Keller, 1997, 49)

4.3 Quality Management

The overall aim of quality management is the planning of a series of key factors to be set into an appropriate context in order to obtain optimum strategy results. (Lieb, 1997, in Pompl, Dreyer, 1997, 34)

RITCHIE and CROUCH distinguish six managerial requirements to be most important in order to increase experienced quality and render a destination competitive: (Brent, Crouch, 1997, in Keller, 1997, 132)

- The **hedonic dimension** of the experience fundamentally tends to provide a pleasurable visit according to the customer type, by generating excitement or quiet enjoyment in order to create long-term memories.

- The **interactive dimension** of a holiday includes the design of activities offering a high level of sociability and integration. Tourists want to have the opportunity to meet people, other visitors, tourism operators and increasingly, the residents of the destination.
- The **novelty dimension** focuses on the need to provide a certain degree of new experience to repeating customers, but at the same time partly familiar features are expected.
- The **comfort dimension** underlines the visitors' need for both physical and mental relaxation.
- The **safety dimension** becomes more and more important and raises new challenges for destination managers.
- The **stimulation dimension** also refers to destination experiences, but in an active way by means of education and information provided to stimulate the intellectual point of view.

The second point of the listing above reflects the importance of personal interaction, interpersonal relationships and intercultural exchange - an experience quality attribute of tourism. Furthermore the authors point out the need to actively plan and manage the tourism destination according to these dimensions. In other words, nothing is left to chance; opportunities to meet people are planned and a framework for intercultural exchange is consciously created.

4.3.1 Total Quality Management

The aim of TQM is the creation of a holistic view of quality management integrating all aspects and people involved. Qualitative thinking should become a basic attitude of everybody involved in the service providing process. (Lieb, 1997, in Pompl, Dreyer, 1997, 37)
As defined in the norm ISO 8402, (in Pompl, 1997, in Pomple, Dreyer, 1997, 5) TQM is a management style based on the collaboration of all organisation members, that focuses on the customer satisfaction, on long term success as well as on the benefits of employees and society.
ALBRECHT (1993, in Pompl, Dreyer, 1997, 5) proposes a definition for *Total Service Quality* based on the concept above. He argues that it is the condition upon which the organisation

brings the highest benefits to all stakeholders: the customer, owners and employees. In order to elaborate *Total Destination Quality,* the local community, as well as the environment, has to be incorporated.

The figure below shows the modified approach of ALBRECHTS' *Total Service Quality* by adding the above mentioned components. The first group of the local population directly or indirectly involved in tourism also includes owners of tourism businesses everybody benefiting from tourism development in the destination. Another group represents the local population neither directly nor indirectly involved in tourism. The customer component remains and the ecological environment forms the fourth part.

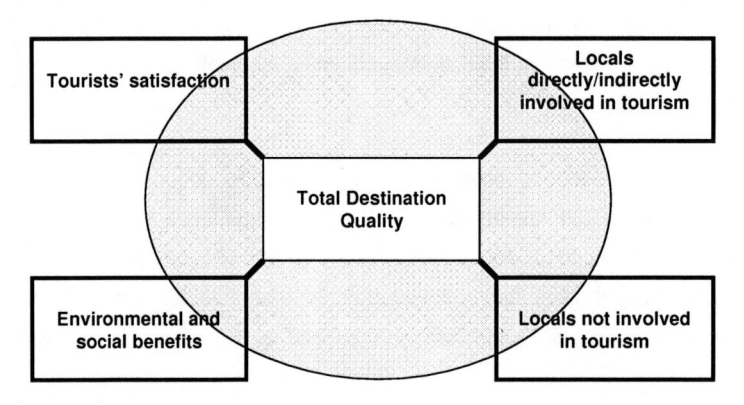

Figure 7: Total Destination Quality[8]

The ecological quality refers to sustainable tourism development with regards to the natural environment of the destination. The social quality component refers to issues concerning the local population. Some examples would be the increase or decrease of quality of life for local people due to additional traffic, increased price levels, lack of involvement in the decision making process and unequal tourism benefits etc.

The TQM applies a top-to-bottom approach assuming that changes have to be initiated and put through by the top management. Without the active participation and role-modelling of management, the TQM can not be realized. (Lieb, 1997, in Pompl, Dreyer, 1997, 38) "People must come to work not only to do their jobs, but also to think about how to improve their jobs. People must be empowered at the lowest possible manner to

---

[8] after Pompl (1997), in Pompl (1997), 5

perform processes in an optimum manner." (Langer, 1997, 2) TQM affects basic rules and values of the company. Modifications on this level take a long time and require commitment and willingness on all hierarchical levels. As a consequence, TQM has to be considered as a "[…] foundation of a continuously improving organization." (Dale, 2003, 1) Some of the most common obstacles that hinder a successful implementation of TQM are proposed by DALE (2003, 10-13)

- Lack of management commitment
- Inability to change the organisational culture
- Lack of continuous training and education
- Ineffective measurement techniques and lack of access to data and results
- Paying inadequate attention to internal and external customers

4.3.2 Integrated Quality Management

"Integrated Quality Management (IQM) focuses on improving visitor satisfaction, while seeking to improve the local economy, the environment and the quality of life of the local community." (European Commission, 1999, 57) Quality Management is a cyclical and continuous concept. In the case of IQM, it follows simple and transparent procedures requiring the collaboration of the entire community "[…] from both the tourism-receptive and tourism-hostile perspective […]" (Youell, 2003, in Hall, 2003, 176).

As shown in the figure below, the overall goal is to create a destination with intact or even improved natural, social and cultural environments, provide benefits without conflicts for the community, customer satisfaction for the visitors and improved performance for tourism enterprises. (European Commission, 1999, 11)

YOUELL (2003, in Hall, 2003, 171-175) recognises the benefits of IQM, especially for rural destinations stating that its' application "[…] has the potential to improve competitiveness within the sector while at the same time safeguarding social, cultural and environmental integrity." One of the core principles of IQM is the concept of sustainability. It accepts the fragility of rural areas, regarding both the environmental as well as the social aspects. A main objective is therefore the preservation or even improvement of the destination's environment in order to respond to the tourists' demand of unspoilt nature and a healthy environment.

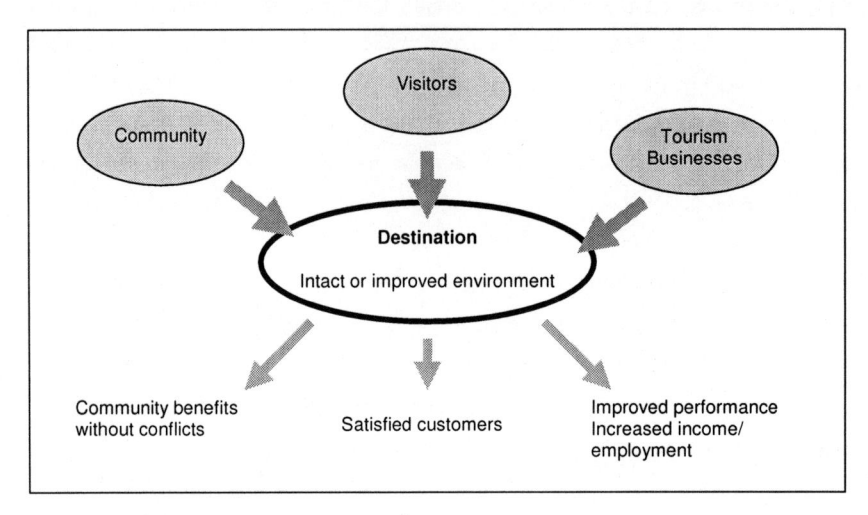

Figure 8: Integrated Quality Management[9]

The methodology of IQM proposes a multiple phase approach. It starts with getting to know visitors' needs, setting standards, continuous feedback from visitors, tourism businesses and the local population. The next step is to make improvements and check impacts. The IQM tends to involve the entire community, directly or indirectly involved in tourism in order to improve the overall quality of the destination. Objectives of IQM defined by the EUROPEAN COMMISSION (1999, 22) are: the reduction of visitor pressure on fragile environments, assistance of traditional industries through tourism, providing the visitors with an authentic experience of heritage, rural life, culture and traditions.

IQM, often considered as an adaptation of TQM, can help destination managers to combine their twin objectives. On one side, increasing local income and employment is a main goal, while on the other side the natural, social and cultural environment has to be protected from the negative impacts of tourism. (Youell, 2003, in Hall, 2003, 173) It therefore has to focus on these two main aspects. Visitor satisfaction and expectations for improvement of quality of life of the local population are always based on the involvement of local community members throughout the entire process.

The main concepts applied in the IQM approach are community integration in the planning and strategy finding process and the quality delivery during all phases of a tourism service.

---

[9] European Commission (1999), 11

Furthermore, the integration of all industries in tourism is crucial in order to provide benefits for other economic sectors. An important factor is the detailed knowledge of visitors' needs and wishes, as well as the satisfaction of both. Training is another key issue of IQM, referring to education and training programs for everybody involved in tourism. Finally, impact monitoring and controlling of management efficiency are included in the IQM process.

Due to the structure of rural tourism, characterised by dispersed and small businesses, the need for effective coordination and leadership in the implementation process of IQM is evident. An ample variety of offers characterises the industry and makes the implementation of uniform quality standards a difficult task. Often, the appeal of tourism businesses is their uniqueness, hence the opposite to uniformity and standardisation. The question to be answered is: can tourist services involving different persons be standardised? (Youell, 2003, in Hall, 2003, 172)

Conclusion

Quality is a key issue for tourism. This chapter tends to give a theoretic overview on different concepts of quality, the characteristics, and the various dimensions of quality in tourism.

Interpersonal contact is a crucial element in tourism. The distinction has been made between contact with local people in the destination and relations among tourists. Contact in any form is considered to be a value-added factor, with a high influence on the overall perceived quality. The quality of a service includes a series of dimensions, such as the perceived quality of the customer. Others can be boiled down to: sustainability factors, economic, ecological and social dimensions of quality. Commonly, quality is evaluated from the tourist's point of view. This approach does not reflect the total quality of a tourism product. The concept of Total Quality Management reflects the position of all stakeholders involved in a production process. A further step takes into consideration the concept of TDQ which means applying the TQM approach to an entire destination.

As a last theoretic approach, the Integrated Quality Management is presented. This method calls for the local community of a tourism destination to be involved in the planning and decision making process and to actively take part in the destination management process. The IQM is based on the framework of sustainable development, hence it is a recommendable management approach for rural tourism destinations.

5 THE INTEGRATION OF SOCIAL AND CULTURAL ASPECTS IN A QUALITY MANAGEMENT SYSTEM

In order to compete on the global market, quality has become a major issue in all industries. Companies invest high amounts of money in quality improvement and controlling tools. These concepts mostly focus on the product quality, the service quality and, ever more often, the environmental quality. Despite the increasing importance of social and cultural aspects, especially in the field of tourism, there has not been much research conducted to develop new concepts and methodologies. As often argued, there is an absence of longitudinal studies of communities affected by tourism. On the other hand, the idea that "if carefully planned and managed, tourism can help conserve the environmental and cultural heritage of an area" (WTO, 1993, 105) is no more called in dispute.

In chapter two, certain quality management issues of tourism have been discussed. This part focuses on the quality of social and cultural aspects in tourism. It is crucial to examine different points of view and to consider all stakeholders with equal importance. During the first approach, social and cultural quality for the local population has to be ensured in order to simultaneously improve the experience quality of the tourists. The quality of the tourist experience and tourist satisfaction can be measured by conducting satisfaction surveys. The measure of satisfaction of the host population and social and cultural quality are often neglected.

Before starting with the analysis of quality management tools, strategies and theories, two fundamental questions have to be posed:

> Shall social and cultural aspects be managed?
> Can social and cultural aspects be managed?

This work can not propose a definite answer to these questions as there is *no* satisfactory and concrete response. Those questions have to be illuminated from different points of view and according to every single specific situation.

There is a series of arguments why social and cultural aspects can not be managed: there is no appropriate definition, they are subjective and heterogeneous, the issues are complex, there is a lack of information and methodology and lack of interest from part of the stakeholders, just to mention a few.

It is not the idea to apply quality management with the objective to increase visitor numbers and economic benefits for stakeholders in the tourism industry. The goal is to apply measures to increase social and cultural quality for the local community and as a consequence for the tourists. Benefits can be improved, relationships between tourists and hosts, less conflict within the community (between some members of the local community favouring, and others rejecting tourism development), enhanced cooperation on the destination level, improved quality of life for the local population, revitalisation of cultural development and enriched experiences for tourists and hosts.

The quality of the tourist experience is based on interaction with people. The quality of contact with others constitutes an added value. There are many occasions for contact with other tourists, service providers and local community members. Only local people satisfied with their quality of life and with the ongoing tourism development can positively react to or interact with tourists and make them feel welcome and appreciated. The figure below illustrates this relationship of tourists and hosts in form of a symbiosis. The local community benefits from tourism through increased quality of life, revitalisation of the community, protection of cultural heritage or enrichment through social contacts. Their positive attitude towards tourism is directly transmitted to the tourists. This sensitive relationship is highly influenced by the external environment in which it takes place.

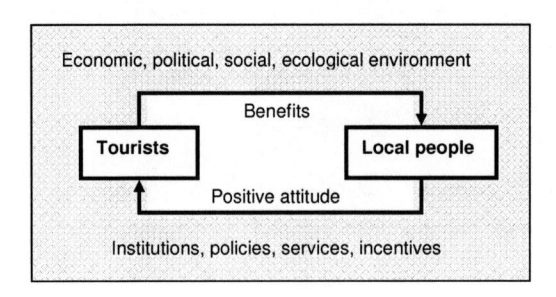

Figure 9: Social contacts model between tourists and hosts[10]

In general, public authorities have not yet realised the importance of the human resource factor, in other words people working in tourism but also the local population in general.

---

[10] elaboration by the author

Managerial actions to improve this relationship remain very sporadic, depending on small-scale initiatives. Also the concept of TQM discussed earlier, stresses the importance of the involvement and satisfaction of all stakeholders as a key factor for success.

In terms of standardisation, control of interpersonal contacts and regulated cultural development, the objective can not be management as it would be contradictory to the principals of sustainable development, such as authenticity, involvement and empowerment of the local population. The impact assessment and the evaluation of the situation in order to create a favourable environment and framework that fosters an appropriate development and balanced intercultural exchange are of primary importance.

5.1 Impact assessment models

Any form of tourism has an impact on the host communities, therefore impact assessment models and tools are crucial for future planning. When studying social and cultural impacts, numeric data is not appropriate and researchers mainly rely on qualitative data. In literature, models are provided in order to analyse and illustrate the effects of tourism on the host population. Nevertheless, the following concepts remain theoretic and only produce synthesised, schematic pictures of social impacts of tourism development.

5.1.1 Doxeys' irritation model

The model proposed by DOXEY (1975) establishes an index of irritation reflecting the attitude of the local population towards tourism. The degree of irritation among the residents of a destination caused by the accumulated effects of tourism development increases proportionally with the growing number of tourists. (Izquierdo, Salas, 1999, 199) In literature, it is often referred to as *Irritex*. DOXEY developed a causal model that illustrates the effects of growing tourism on the attitude of local community members towards tourists. The model was initially developed in the context of mass tourism in saturated tourism destinations. (Howforth, Munt, 1998, 249)

As illustrated in the following figure, DOXEY distinguishes four stages of irritation that occur when the number of tourists increases in a destination. Each level of irritation is characterised by certain behavioural patterns and perceptions: (Howforth, Munt, 1998, 249, Manson, 2003, 47, Page, Dowling, 2002, 173)

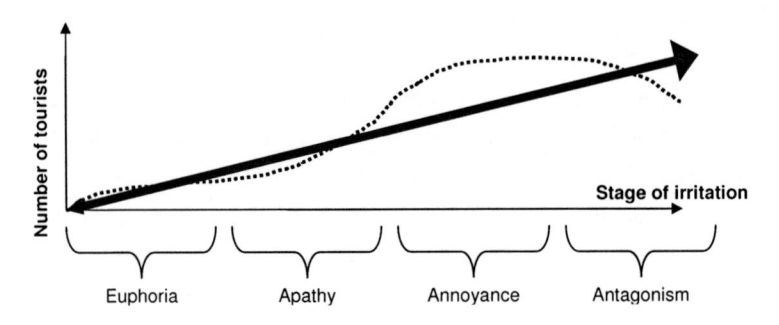

Integration of social and cultural aspects in a management system

Figure 10: Doxeys' index of irritation[11]

The first stage is characterised by euphoric behaviour of the local population towards few tourists that come to visit an unspoilt and unexploited destination. It's the initial phase of tourism development, and both tourists, as well as investors, are welcome.

Following the stage of euphoria, feelings of apathy emerge when the number of visitors increases and tourist flow is taken for granted. The first delight about the arrival of tourists fades, and contact between hosts and visitors becomes more formal and commercial. People realise the economic importance of tourism and successfully sell their destination.

The next stage is marked by annoyance, the saturation point of the destination is approached. Local protest begins to take form, first complaints and misgivings emerge in the local community. People start to feel the social, environmental and cultural pressure that affects the community.

The last level of irritation is defined as stage of antagonism in which irritation and rejection are expressed openly; the local population has completely changed their attitude and considers the visitors to be responsible for problems and mishaps in their community. On the other side, promotion has to be increased in order to offset the deteriorated reputation of the destination.

The model was developed to be unidirectional, which means that once the last stage is reached, the local population will try everything to change or stop the development of tourism. According to several commentators, DOXEYS' model can not be considered to be simply unidirectional. On the contrary, attitudes of the host population towards tourism change throughout the destination's lifecycle. Attitudes may also change on a seasonal basis. At the beginning of the season, tourists are highly welcomed but with increasing number and towards the end of the season, this attitude changes. Hence DOXEYS' model

---

[11] elaboration by the author

has to be modified. An additional phase has to be added, "nostalgia". The feeling of "the good old times" comes up when the level of irritation starts to decline due to sinking numbers of tourists. (Boyne, 2003, in Hall, 2003, 30f)

5.1.2 Getz study

Some of the most important studies intending to apply theoretic models on destinations were conducted by GETZ. He proposed an additional development of DOXEY'S' model of host irritation. GETZ suggested that the attitudes of residents towards tourists don't change greatly over time, as DOXEY had argued, but are rather sensible to economic fluctuations. Furthermore, the attitude towards tourism varies among different groups of people. Local community members directly involved in tourism would therefore have a more positive view than people not or only indirectly benefiting of the development of tourism. Also, socio-demographic factors play an important role in the perception of tourism. According to GETZ'S study. in general young people are more in favour of tourism and new development. (Manson, 2003, 49) One has to consider the understanding of "attitude" as a "state of mind of the individual towards a value" (Allport, 1996, in Page, 2002, 172) Therefore as GETZ stated, attitudes are reinforced by the way individuals and groups perceive reality.

5.1.3 Ap and Crompton's model

Furthermore AP and CROMPTON argue that a community affected by the development of tourism can not be considered as a homogeneous group, but on the contrary is characterised by a variety of stakeholders' interests and attitudes. As suggested by AP and CROMPTON, those different views can be divided into four groups, of which each one shares common opinions and attitudes.

The first group is characterised by embracement and eagerly welcomes tourists. Most likely residents directly involved and benefiting from tourism development will form this group. Tolerance is the prevailing attitude of the second group, they demonstrate a certain degree of ambivalence towards tourism. There are equal elements of tourism they appreciate and dislike. The third group of residents adjusts their lifestyles to tourism, for example they are willing or forced to reschedule their activities in order to avoid crowds.

The last part of the local population completely rejects the development of tourism and withdraws temporarily from the community. (Page, Dowling, 2002, 173)

5.1.4 Butler's model

Butler's model analyses the attitude and behaviour of the local population towards the development of tourism in the destination, applying a two axes model. The attitudes are classified as positive or negative on one axis and active or passive behaviour is shown on the second axis. (Izquierdo, Salas, 1999, 199) Thanks to this model, Butler intended to develop an approach to illustrate the influence of tourism according to the different ways in which the local population reacted.

Attitude / Behaviour

	Positive	Negative
Active	Aggressive promotion of tourism	Manifestation against tourism development
Passive	Silent acceptation of tourism	Resignation of opposition of tourism

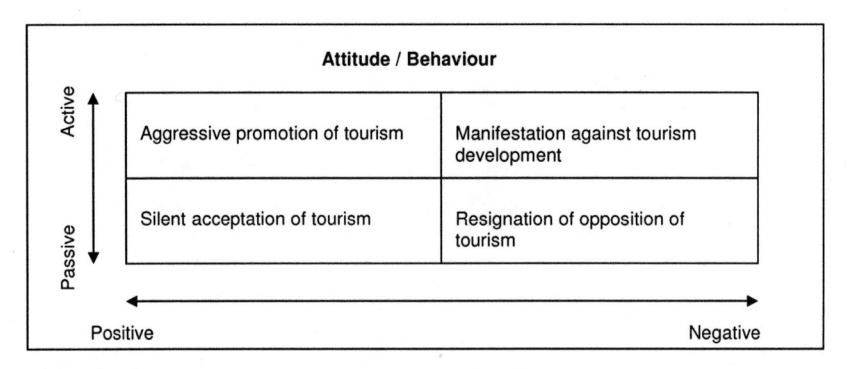

Figure 11: Butler's Attitude / Behaviour model[12]

As illustrated in the figure above, BUTLER proposes a scale of attitudes towards tourism with two extreme values; positive and negative. The attitude of the population or a specific interest group can be determined and presented on this scale. Furthermore, the behaviour of the population has to be classified on a scale between passive and active. By applying this concept and analysing the position of all interest groups in a destination, a general picture of the destination's attitude and reaction towards tourism can be derived.

---

[12] Izquierdo, Salas (1999), 199

5.1.5 Evaluation of cultural impacts

In most literature regarding this issue, social and cultural impacts are treated jointly as socio-cultural impacts. No specific evaluation techniques of cultural aspects have therefore been presented so far. MELLO and SUSA (in Izquierdo, Salas, 1999, 201) point out that cultural elements are assimilated, substituted and transformed over time as a natural and positive process of evolution. On the other side, actions are taken to ensure the recuperation and preservation of traditional cultural elements as a contraposition to the homogenisation of culture, the process of *acculturation* and cultural loss. An analysis of cultural impacts, such as a qualitative observation including all internal and external processes affecting cultural development: economic, political, environmental and social factors, has to hence be realised. Most commonly used methods to obtain information on the perception of the local population are household surveys, focus groups, town hall meetings, interviews and questionnaires.

According to MATHIESON and WALL (1990, in Izquierdo, Salas, 1999, 201), the evaluation of cultural impacts of tourism has to at least have the following three aspects of culture as a focus:

a. Specifically animated forms of culture that include important elements for the host society, such as religious ceremonies, popular manifestations, folklore and rites.
b. Forms of culture that are reflected in the destination area, for example consumer behaviour, specific language use, alimentary characteristics, etc., referring to key elements for the survival of a local culture.
c. Forms of culture that are not animated or *material culture* referring to architecture, craftworks and arts

5.1.6 General impact assessment model

Besides the methods for the assessment of specific effects of tourism, POTTER (1978, in Page, Dowling, 2002, 150) elaborated a general methodology of impact assessment. This method follows nine steps towards a decision and planning for the minimisation of negative impacts. This assessment model is based on expert opinions and knowledge. In order to make it a viable method, a Delphi questionnaire is recommended to combine and contrast various expert opinions.

The concept consists of a scenario approach with different variables. In the first step, the context of tourism in the destination is analysed. The environmental, social and economic environment is analysed assuming that tourism will continue to grow. A second approach is the prediction of the environment assuming tourism will not continue. The next step analyses the nature of tourism, the type of tourism developed in the destination and how tourism will change in the future. Finally the future perspectives are analysed, compared and actions to be taken are defined.

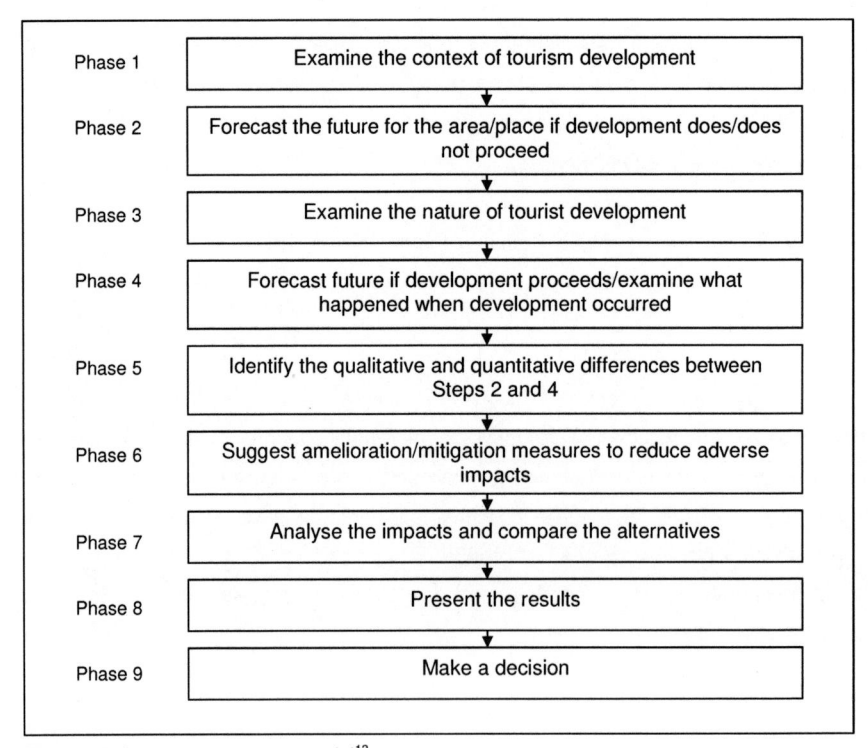

Phase 1	Examine the context of tourism development
Phase 2	Forecast the future for the area/place if development does/does not proceed
Phase 3	Examine the nature of tourist development
Phase 4	Forecast future if development proceeds/examine what happened when development occurred
Phase 5	Identify the qualitative and quantitative differences between Steps 2 and 4
Phase 6	Suggest amelioration/mitigation measures to reduce adverse impacts
Phase 7	Analyse the impacts and compare the alternatives
Phase 8	Present the results
Phase 9	Make a decision

Figure 12: Impact assessment model[13]

---

[13] Potter (1978), in Page, Dowling (2002), 150

Conclusion

The assessment of social and cultural impacts of tourism is a complex task as "it is usually impossible to filter out other influences". (Smith, 2003, 55) Nevertheless, research in this field is essential in order to ensure a sustainable development of tourism in the long term. Very general and different techniques can be used in order to obtain information on the influences perceived by the local population itself. "Household surveys or questionnaires, focus group interviews, participant observation, or methods such as the Delphi Technique" (Smith, 2003, 55) are the most commonly used in this context.

DOXEYS' model is the most referred to in literature but has no practical viability. It can only be used as a theoretic concept for further social impact research. Every single concept has its correctness and attempts to provide a framework. BUTLERS' model is very interesting as it tends to create a general impression of predominant attitudes and reactions in a destination.

The most important critique concerning Doxeys' model, as well as others based on tourist numbers, is not reflected in common literature. The irritation caused by the first tourists and foreigners coming to a destination is completely neglected. The irritation caused by first contact with tourists is extremely high among the local population. Only after a certain time of adjustment and acceptance of the new situation, small numbers of tourists are welcomed and appreciated. As Doxeys' model was initially developed for mature destinations, this pre-stage was left apart but it certainly has a high importance in virgin and unexploited destinations.

Cultural aspects are very rarely explicitly assessed and are usually integrated within the scope of socio-cultural impact models. Nevertheless, they should not be neglected as culture is a major component of tourism and society.

5.1.7 Social impact model

The figure below is an attempt to develop a general model for social impacts, illustrating the attitudes of different interest groups within the local population towards tourism. The model tends to integrate the key issues of the models developed by DOXEY, GETZ, AP AND CROMPTON and BUTLER which were presented at the beginning of this chapter. The vertical axis shows a continuous scale from a highly negative to highly positive attitude towards tourism development; the horizontal axis reflects the timeline. The black curve illustrates the destinations' life cycle with an introduction phase, a growth stage, maturity, decline and rejuvenation. The horizontal line in the middle indicates a neutral attitude towards tourism.

1	Destination life cycle
2	Local people directly involved in tourism
3	Local people benefiting from tourism
4	Local people tolerant towards tourism
5	Local people refusing tourism

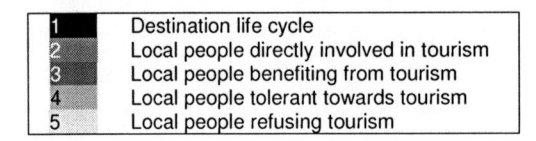

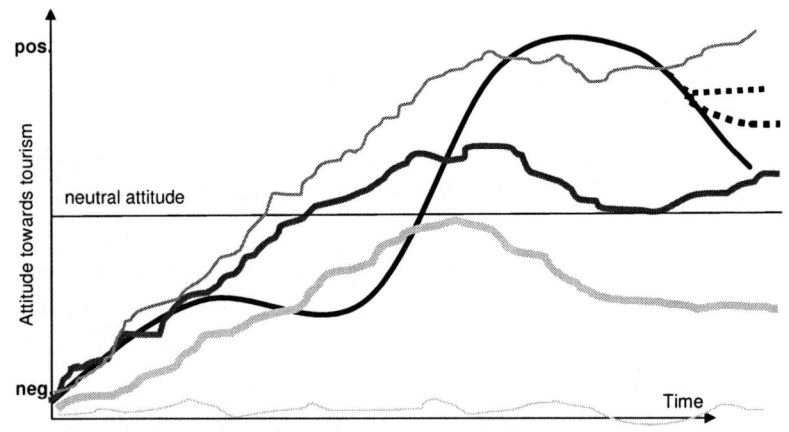

Figure 13: Social Impact Model[14]

The concept of attitudes changing over time, introduced by DOXEY, is reflected in the model above, however it is no longer a unidirectional concept but a continuously changing one. GETZ proposed the dependency of attitudes on economic fluctuations and the notion that attitudes vary among different groups with respect to their interest in tourism. The economic development of tourism is reflected in the life cycle of the destination, hence it constitutes the basis for the model above. Also, AP AND CROMPTON defined various groups within the local population that show different attitudes towards tourism, depending on the benefits they receive.

Line "2" shows the generally very positive attitude of local people who are directly involved in tourism and gain high benefits. After a certain period of reluctance at the beginning, they realise that tourism generates economic benefits and their attitude improves. Their general attitude is hence very positive, despite certain seasonal variations. Also, when maturity is reached the high level of euphoria is maintained as high benefits are generated. This

---

[14] after Doxey, Getz, Butler, Ap and Crompton

attitude can even increase at the beginning of the decline phase when fewer tourists come to the destination. Line "3" reflects the attitude of people being tolerant and having a generally positive feeling towards the development of tourism. They indirectly profit from tourism and believe it to have positive effects on the destination. Nevertheless, in the maturity stage they realise that tourism also creates negative impacts and so become less euphoric about it. When tourist arrivals start to decline, these people move into a stage of nostalgia and their attitude towards tourists improves again. Curve "4" represents the attitude of local people not involved in tourism, they realise certain positive influences during the growth stage as their quality of life improves, but become very reluctant towards tourism when the first negative impacts become evident. Line "5" illustrates the last group of local people, those who completely refuse any form of tourism.

The weight of the curves indicates the proportional size of each of the different groups within a destination. In the presented case, the majority of local people doesn't show extreme attitudes, but is generally either neutral, slightly in favour or against tourism.

5.2 Management and planning tools for tourism impacts

Managing and planning of tourism is crucial in order to minimise negative impacts and maximise benefits for hosts, tourists and other stakeholders. The traditional view of tourism planning is planning in favour of tourism, it focuses on a numeric growth and development of tourism. Main objectives such as the increase in tourist arrivals, capacities and economic benefits are commonly strived for. (Page, Dowling, 2002, 197) Throughout the last decades, the goals of tourism planning have changed and other aspects have become important for the management of a tourist destination. Tourism managers now understand the necessity of long-term planning and the importance of its integration in a wider political, economic, social and environmental framework. (Dowling, Fennell, 2003, in Fennell, 2003, 8)
Tourism has been an uncontrolled and unplanned growing industry and has only recently become a field worth studying.

Management leads people towards a common objective or, as defined by PAGE and DOWLING (2002, 227), "[...] management is about how things are done and the process of organising other people to undertake tasks towards common goals." MC LENNAN (1987, in

Page, Dowling, 2002, 195) defines the four main principal activities of management: planning, organisation, leadership and control. Furthermore he describes planning to be the goal setting process where objectives are defined and at the same time, the methods of how to achieve them are planned. According to DOWLING and FENNELL (2003, in Fennell, 2003, 6) planning "[...] requires some estimated perception of the future" which is obtained by observation and deduction of research. Furthermore "planning should provide a resource for informed decision making". Summarising, one can say that planning means the process leading to the definition of objectives. HALL (2000, in Fennell, 2003, 6) argued that planning was part of a process he termed the "planning–decision–action process".

Management is the overall task coordinating the entire process and bringing all stakeholders to agree on a consensus, hence the challenge of management is "achieving a balance between each of their needs and the viable development [...]" (Page, 2002, 196) of the local tourism industry. This task is especially difficult as stakeholders in tourism range from public authorities, non-governmental organisations, private enterprises, interest groups and associations to local residents, and each group has specific interests, opinions and demands. BACKMAN (Petrick, Wright, 2001, in Weaver, 2001, 453) brings the problem to the point by stating that tourism "suffers from the problem of everybody's business is nobody's business". The dispersion of interests and involvement in the tourism sector easily lead to a fragmentation of efforts and resources, involve high risk potential and, in general, lacks synergies and efficiency.

Tourism is a multi-stakeholder industry involving different activities. Therefore a crucial question is: on which level planning should be done? As often stated in literature, public bodies have to take the responsibility of planning as "[...] these bodies should be able to take a holistic perspective [...] of wider issues for a destination". (Page, Dowling, 2002, 196f) Tourism can not be seen as an isolated phenomenon but has to be considered in the context of the destination, its natural, economic and social environment. It is therefore crucial that tourism development is integrated in a *total resource analysis* (Page, Dowling, 2002, 197) and general development plan of the area.

Tourism planning has to be carried out on various levels, from the broadest level to the smallest tourism business. The planning on the intra-national level has had increasing importance, referring to two or more countries forming a region and working together. (Pearce, 1989, in Page, Dowling, 2002, 208) On the national level, a series of issues are treated, such as the designation of tourist regions and major tourist attractions, access and transport to and within the country, future development and national policies. Regional planning deals with the transport network within the region, specific tourist resorts, sites and attractions, the incorporation of economic, ecologic and social concerns in a regional set of policies, land distribution and development of tourism destinations. (Dowling, Fennell, 2003, in Fennell, 2003, 9) On a local level, more specific topics are planned such as local attractions, marketing of the site, environmental, social and cultural issues. The distribution of tasks and responsibilities depends on the political structure of a country. Cooperation between different countries or regions can enhance interdisciplinary planning of tourism concerning specific projects. "It is important to distinguish between the management roles" [...] of the different tourism agencies and "the specific management responsibilities" (Page, Dowling, 2002, 198)

Worth a consideration is the appropriate timing of tourism planning. HALL (2000, in Page, Dowling, 2002, 196) argues that:

> demands for tourism planning and government intervention in the development process are typically a response to the unwanted effects of tourism development at the local level. The rapid pace of tourism growth and development, the nature of tourism itself and the corresponding absence of single agency responsibilities for tourism related development has often meant that public sector responses to the impacts of tourism on destination has often been ad hoc, rather than predetermined strategies oriented towards development objectives.

Planning today is still confused with crisis management. Planning in situations of crisis becomes a spontaneous process in order to stop, slow down or reverse undesired effects of tourism which have become obvious, hence the goal of crisis management is to satisfy instantly an urgent need without having taken the time for long-term observation and in-depth analysis of the problem. On the contrary, planning as defined earlier is a process "which aims to anticipate, regulate and monitor change so as to contribute to the wider sustainability of the destination, and thereby enhance the tourist experience of the destination or place." (Page, Dowling, 2002, 196f)

Tourism planning, like any other planning process, should be "a continuous process, systems oriented, integrated within the overall planning of an area, include environmental and community considerations, and be pragmatic in application" (Page, Dowling, 2002, 198) MURPHY (1985, in Fennell, 2003, 7) pointed out the importance of the integration of social factors in restructured tourism planning in a way that "[...] environmental and social factors may be placed alongside economic considerations". PEARCE (1989, in Page, Dowling, 2002, 209) defined the general planning goals for tourism as a harmonious development of the area creating an appropriate "[...] balance between and among different sectors in terms of capacity, quality and style as well as compatibility of different functions". The importance of planning becomes evident considering the fact that "unplanned, uncontrolled tourism growth can destroy the very resource on which it is built" (Pearce 1989, in Fennell, 2003, 6)

5.2.1 Planning process

Planning is "[...] organising the future to achieve certain objectives". (WTO, 2001, 42) It gives a guideline for actions to be taken, decisions to be made and how to allocate resources in order to reach a well defined goal. In literature, a series of planning approaches is defined that respond to different planning strategies and focus on specific issues.
The WTO (2001, 42f) proposes six approaches for the planning of sustainable tourism. The "continuous and flexible approach", which is adapted to changing situations, the "comprehensive approach", the "integrated approach" where tourism planning forms part of a global planning process, "environmental and sustainable approach", "community based approach", which focuses on the integration of the local population in the planning process, the "implementable approach" concentrating on implementation techniques and the "strategic planning approach" coping with urgent issues. The knowledge of these approaches can not be considered as a step by step guideline, but rather gives directions of how a planning process can be set up.

Managing is the process of "[...] organizing resources and opportunities for other people, for the purpose of meeting their needs" and (Fennell, Dowling, 2003, in Fennell, 2003, 340) can be split up in five well defined planning phases:

- **Project planning**: creation of a vision and mission statement, definition of common goals, strategies and measures
- **Needs and assets**: analysis of the customers' motives, needs and wants and the elaboration of an inventory of attractions (natural, cultural, historical and architectonical)
- **Project design**: includes the detailed planning of the project course and risk management

- **Project implementation**: deals with all issues regarding the realisation of the project, such as marketing, budgeting, public relations, implementation strategies
- **Evaluation**: consist of a series of evaluation models in order to decide on how to assess the project

COCCOSSIS and MEXA (2004, in Coccossis, 2004, 76) even propose a more detailed planning approach. During a research pre-phase the physical, ecological, socio-cultural, political-economic and institutional environment of the tourism destination are analysed in the framework of a broader context including trends, future prospects, national strategies and policies. As a next step, a SWOT analysis is conducted in order to identify strengths, weaknesses, opportunities and threats of the destination. As a following step, goals and objectives are formulated according to the identified characteristics of the destination and specific priorities, the elaboration of alternatives and different options. Once a preferable course of action has been chosen, a common strategy has to be formulated followed by a detailed strategy to prevent difficulties in the implementation phase. After the implementation phase, monitoring and evaluation of the outcomes are necessary in order to allow continuous improvement. Objectives should be couched in terms that are measurable, result-oriented, and time dependent. They should address the concepts of effectiveness, efficiency and equity and form the base of project evaluation. (Backman, Petrick, Wright, 2001, in Weaver, 2001, 457)

Choosing a multi-organisational approach (in other words, involving different organisations and groups in the planning process) can result more cost and time-effective as well as more efficient in the treatment of information due to the positive effects of multi-disciplinary cooperation. (Backman, Petrick, Wright, 2001, in Weaver, 2001, 455)

5.2.2 The tourism management spectrum

The tourism management spectrum proposed by JIM (1989, in Page, Dowling, 2002, 216) gives an overview of the scale of influence a manager can have on tourism development. Appropriate measures have to be decided on, depending on the specific objectives, the degree of deterioration, as well as on the pace of progress.

The measures may range from influencing tourist behaviour and conduct over changing the use of land and type of tourism in the area, to access limitation for tourists to specific attractions or entire areas.

Measures	Management objectives	Techniques
Soft Influencing use behaviour	To change user attitudes and behaviour towards environment, local population and culture in order to reduce negative impacts.	Using environmental information and education programs Establishment of a code of ethics/conduct
Intermediate Redistributing use	To reduce the contrast between heavily used and lightly used areas over time To redistribute land uses so that activities are practiced in appropriate areas	Land use planning Planning of tourism development Concentration versus dispersion
Hard Rationing use	Controlling tourist numbers relative to type, place and time To lower access levels to match carrying capacities	Limitation of access to tourism sites Differential pricing, fees, and queuing Advanced reservation by permit

Table 2: The tourism management spectrum[15]

5.2.3 Local participation

The importance of the host community as a major player in decision-making and tourism planning has been increasingly recognised among tourism managers and scientists. (Manson, 2003, 117) According to the WTO (2001, 131) community involvement in tourism is an important planning tool in order to "[...] reinforce positive impacts and mitigate negative ones [...]".
Nevertheless one has to keep in mind that a community is a heterogeneous group of people with different opinions, attitudes, and behaviours, hence there is no such thing as *the* host community. The attitude of the local population towards tourism can decide upon success or failure of tourism development in a destination. One key element of tourism is the contact between visitors and visited. The intercultural exchange is one of the crucial factors of consumer satisfaction in tourism. Any hostile behaviour of members of the host community towards tourists can destroy the standing of a destination in the long-term and

---
[15] after Jim (1989), in Page, Dowling (2002), 216

not even high investments in promotion and marketing can make undo or reverse negative opinions.

As MOWFORTH and MUNT (1998, in Manson, 2003, 118) argued, one of the main criteria for achieving sustainability is the participation of local people. Nevertheless the involvement of local communities does not necessarily guarantee the success of projects and of tourism development. The right approach, project planning and professional carrying out are key elements and have high influence on the outcome of the project. The integration of the local residents in the project planning process has a series of benefits. The most evident is that through the information provided by the local community and its integration in the decision making phase, conflicts are brought up and can be resolved at an early stage. This reduces the chance of failure of the entire project. (Backman, Petrick, Wright, 2001, in Weaver, 2001, 457)

According to the World Bank Participation Sourcebook (1998, in Wearing, 2001, in Weaver, 2001, 398), the term *Participatory Rural Appraisal* stands for "a growing family of participatory approaches and methods that emphasize local knowledge and enable local people to elaborate their own appraisal, analysis and plans." Furthermore, PRA "enables communities to monitor and evaluate the results of these initiatives". (The Institute of Development Studies, 1996). It is a process of multidisciplinary participation, mobilisation and integration of different groups. The main objective is to gather information and practical knowledge of people who are integrated in the entire project. PRA can initiate and enhance collaboration on a local level as stakeholders have "[...] a buy-in and a degree of empowerment [...]" (Page, Dowling, 2002, 224) in the process of tourism development.

IZQUIERDO and SALAS (1999, 92) define the participative planning as a process of social learning. Of major importance is the coordination and collaboration between professionals and local people in a joint learning process in which planning is carried out by linking theoretical and scientific knowledge with the practical and specific information local people can provide.
Still, there is not much evidence of cases where local participation has been effective and successful in the implementation of tourism. MANSON (2003, 119) states that one of the main reasons for failure is the fact that a thing such as *a community* simply doesn't exist in reality, hence the development of a consensus supported by the entire community is virtually impossible.

SWARBROOKE (2004, 33) mentions another important aspect, saying that the involvement of the local population provides "[...] an opportunity for a minority of self-appointed community spokespeople, or people with strong views to dominate the process. It might occur that the opinion of the community is ignored or underestimated by professionals when their own ideas differ from those of the population. Conflicts that come up during a participatory debate can hold on also when the official part is over. Or, seen the other way round, old conflicts among certain participants can hinder or even stop the process of local participation. It can also be that people are not interested in participating in such a planning process. There are cases in which enhancing the awareness of the local population has led to increased cautiousness and concern, and finally direct participation. (WTO, 1993, 114)

JERKINS (1993, in Manson, 2003, 120) defines seven obstacles causing difficulties in the process of local participation in tourism planning:

a. The public in general has difficulties in understanding complex and technical planning issues.
b. The public does not necessarily understand how the planning process operates or how decisions are made.
c. Apathy amongst some, if not a majority, of citizens.
d. The problem of attaining and maintaining the representation of all views in a decision making process.
e. The increased cost in relation to staff time and money.
f. The fact that decision making takes much longer
g. The overall efficiency of the decision making process is adversely affected.

Reviewing the arguments stated above, it becomes clear that the main difficulties are related to the communication and transmission of information as well as the understanding of technical issues. The points "*a*", "*b*" and "*c*" can be resolved, or at least reduced, by extensive communication between the experts leading the project and the population. The more information people have at their disposal, the better they can argue and the faster the decision will be taken. The argument "*c*" is somewhat special and initiates a discussion about whether a project should be put through despite the apathy of certain groups of the local community. Point "*d*" refers to the question of participation in general and the willingness of community members to scarifice their time in order to take part in the process. One can argue that enough information and the interest of people in their living environment should be strong motivational factors. On the other hand, this argument refers to the difficulties in distinguishing the different opinions in a community and integrating all of them in the decision making process. The last three arguments are not deniable, but they can easily be reduced to a minimum. The fact that a participative decision taking process takes longer and involves higher costs than an expert decision is evident. But the advantage of achieving a consensus, agreement and commitment of the community is still an important investment. The argument that the participative decision making process is less efficient might be true, but furthermore the phase of information and persuasion of the local people affected by tourism development can be considered as unnecessary and one can count on cooperation of all parts.

Besides the obstacles that occur due to the actual participatory process, a series of external factors might influence the decision. Any decisions have to be situated in a framework of governmental policies, legal restrictions and funding options. Furthermore, the power of the tourism industry and the power of external stakeholders in the area play an important role. Economies dependent on tourism don't have absolute freedom of choice. (Swarbrooke, 2004, 34) Participation can occur on different levels and throughout various phases of a project. In general literature, seven levels of participation are distinguished as illustrated in the figure below.

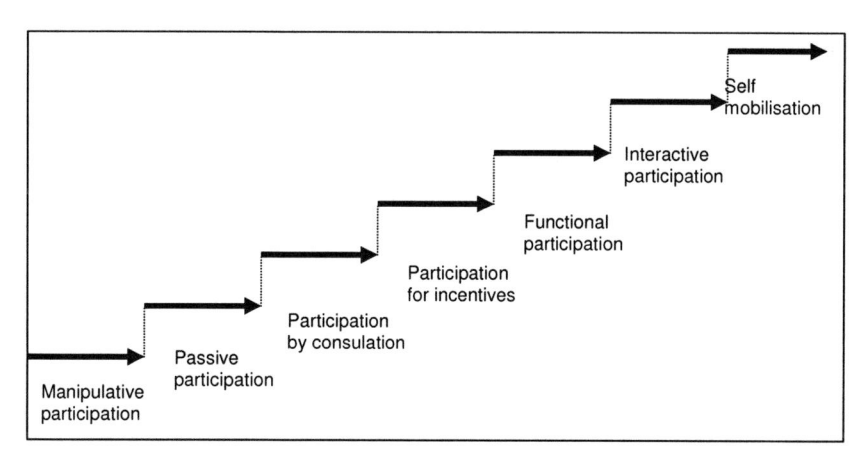

Figure 14: Levels of Participation[16]

---

[16] workshop for DRP (2004)

Each level of participation responds to certain characteristics and different degrees and forms of involvement of the local population. PRETTY created the following typology of participation (Pretty, 1995, in Manson, 2003, 119)

1. **Manipulative participation**: Participation is the mere presence of unelected representatives of the population without any power.
2. **Passive participation**: Information transmitted from the project management to the public without taking into consideration the opinion of the local population. Decisions are taken on the management level; the information belongs to external professionals.
3. **Participation by consultation**: People are consulted or asked to provide information and/or opinions according to a predefined process. The project management is under no obligation to take the results into consideration and the local population has no right to participate in the decision making process.
4. **Participation for incentives**: People are willing to participate in a project by providing resources (workforce, field, material, etc.) in exchange for some material or immaterial incentive. They don't have any influence in the project planning or decision making and only participate in specific phases.
5. **Functional participation**: The participation of people is planned by external agents in order to achieve project goals (often to reduce costs). Objective groups are involved in shared decision-making. Secondary decisions are taken within a certain outline, after primary decisions have been taken by external agents.
6. **Interactive participation**: People are involved in all phases of the project in an interactive form. They participate in the analysis, the development of action plans and perceive their participation as their right and a joint learning process. Local people are considered as full members of the project team and have full control of the available resources.
7. **Self mobilisation**: The highest level of participation refers to the participation of external agents in a project carried out by the local population. People take the initiative and complete a project independently. They inquire for help and advice at external institutions but have full control over the project at every moment. This form of participation is only possible when administration and NGOs provide sufficient support.

As stated before, the local population should be involved in the entire project or in different project phases. The degree of participation can vary among different project phases and depends highly on the project management, but also on the population itself, its motivation and its willingness to take own initiatives. An appropriate approach and preparation of the project is crucial in order to carry out common goals successfully.

Several principals of participative methods have to be taken into consideration in order to put through a project of rural appraisal. As a first step, participants have to give up their habitual roles and attitudes. Those who usually talk and tell people how to do things have to listen, respect and learn. Experts have to appreciate other opinions and be willing to accept any solution. Furthermore, methods have to be changed in order to improve the participation process. There are many techniques and methods that help to obtain information needed. The last principle is the exchange of ideas, opinions and knowledge. Professionals have to be willing to hand on and transmit their technical knowledge to ordinary people.

The following steps can serve as a guideline for the planning and fulfilment of participative projects. One of the most important prerequisites when working on local participation is the flexibility to change and modify predefined plans and outlines. (Workshop for DRP, 2004)

- Preparation
- Field work
- Preliminary proposals
- Revision and new approval
- Final Report

The first phase of local participation, the preparation, includes the determination of the role of local participants, the selection of a multidisciplinary project team, the fulfilment of preliminary studies in order to investigate on the economic and social characteristics of the community and the planning of the participation process (degree of participation and appropriate methods).

The initial phase is particularly important as it is often people's first impressions that decide upon their general attitude towards the project. First contact is made with the host community, their opinions, wishes and needs have to be investigated. Interactive exchange of information takes place, external agents give information about the project and technical issues, while members of the destination community provide their knowledge and ideas. The preliminary proposals for future action plans are jointly elaborated by representatives of the local population and external professionals in a process of learning and development. The recommendations are then presented to the public and in an interactive and transparent process discussed, revised and re-evaluated. At the end, an action plan and implementation scheme is worked out with the participation of the entire project team and the results are then presented in a final report.

5.2.4 Tourism Carrying Capacity

The concept of carrying capacity originally derives from the field of ecology and was developed as "[...] an unidisciplinary, one-dimensional perspective [...]" (Mexa, Coccossis, 2004, in Coccossis, 2004, 37) in order to define the number of individuals an ecosystem is able to absorb before collapsing. HARDIN (1977, 1) defined the concept of carrying capacity as "the maximum number of a species that can be supported indefinitely by a particular habitat, allowing for seasonal and random changes, without degradation of the environment and without diminishing carrying capacity in the future".

According to the WTO (1992, in Izquierdo, Salas, 1999, 162) tourism carrying capacity refers to the level of exploitation which an area can support without damaging the physical, economic and socio-cultural environment. It refers to the limits within which tourism can be developed in a certain area without causing negative effects such as saturation, overcrowding and *acculturation* in the present and future. Indicators used to determine the carrying limits of a destination refer to the volume of tourism (tourists per time), the density of tourism (tourists per unity of space) and proportion (tourist per residents). The concept of tourism carrying capacity can be used in the tourism planning process, as a management tool, benchmark or in the decision making process. (Izquierdo, Salas, 1999, 161f)

LINDSAY (1986, in Glasson, Godfrey, Goodey 1995, 2) proposed a formula to explain the concept of carrying capacity which, of course, remains a theoretical concept, but still gives an idea about the high number of variables and the complexity of the carrying capacity concept.

$CC = f(Q, T, N, U, DM, AB)$

CC	Carrying Capacity
Q	Quantity of resources available
T	Tolerance of those resources to visitors' use
N	Actual number of visitors at the site or setting at a specific moment
U	Type of use or visitor activity undertaken in the destination
DM	Design and management of visitor facilities in the setting
AB	Attitude and behaviour of visitors on the site

A rather general but widely accepted definition of TCC is proposed by WEARING and NEIL (1999, in Page, Dowling, 2002, 204) stating it to be "the maximum use of any site without causing negative effects on the resources, reducing visitor satisfaction, or exerting adverse impact upon the society, economy and culture of the area". According to the definition stated above, it is a multidisciplinary concept including physical, environmental, social, cultural, political and economic aspects in order to establish indicators and maximum limits for the optimum utilisation of tourism resources. The so called total carrying capacity is a combination of different types of carrying capacities, using as an upper level the lowest value of the specific thresholds. The most common types of carrying capacity include: (Swarbrooke, 2004, 29)

- **Physical capacity**, referring to the number of tourists that can be accommodated in a destination (total number of beds).
- **Environmental or ecological capacity** indicates the number of tourists a place can accommodate without harming the environment and ecosystem.
- **Economic capacity** defines the number of tourists that can be welcomed before economical problems arise for the local community (e.g. increased land prices, high living costs).
- **Social capacity** is the limit beyond which social disruption and irreversible cultural changes occur.
- **Perceptual capacity** refers to tourist satisfaction and indicates the number of tourists allowed before the tourist experience begins to be adversely affected.
- **Infrastructure capacity**, limiting the number of tourists a destination can welcome according to the infrastructure available.

In specific literature, even a cultural carrying capacity is proposed. It refers to the limits of tourism development leading to a so called "cultural shock". It would make satisfactory contact between tourists and hosts impossible and endanger the cultural development of the local community. Furthermore, it is defined as the level of mutual tolerance between the cultures of visitor and visited. (Izquierdo, Salas, 1999, 164f)

The cultural and social aspects are strongly interrelated and often not distinguishable: both are expressed in qualitative terms, which, to a high extent, depend on subjective measurement and perception. Social and cultural parameters in the assessment of carrying capacity are: change of life-style, sense of identity and social patterns, the alteration of local culture and traditional labour, the behaviour of the local population towards tourists, their degree of resentment and the quality of the tourists' experience. (Coccossis and Mexa, 2004, in Coccossis, 2004, 60)

Furthermore there is a *psychological capacity*, also referred to as "visitor capacity" (Glasson, Gofrey, Goddey 1995, 1) or "perceptual capacity" (Swarbrooke, 2004, 29) that considers the perception of tourists regarding the presence of other tourists. In other words, it means the tourists' perception of crowdedness and saturation in the destination. (Izquierdo, Salas, 1999, 166)

"Capacity levels, expressed as a function of limits can be real or perceived, and may change as a result of functional adaptation, or social intervention through organizational or technological measures." (Coccossis, 2004 in Coccossis, 2004, 5) Limits are therefore not definite, but have to be seen "[…] as a dynamic concept with spatial-temporal characteristics […]." (Coccossis, 2004 in Coccossis, 2004, 12) They change over time, depending on the patterns of growth and the characteristics of the destination. Capacity limits can be augmented by managerial actions, technical improvements and organisational measures. Since the concept of tourism carrying capacity first came up, the focus has changed from a numerical point of view, defining a maximum acceptable number of tourists, towards the idea of achieving and maintaining desirable conditions, "[…] the limits of acceptable change". (Mexa, Coccossis, 2004, in Coccossis 2004, 48)

The measurement and assessment of tourism carrying capacities has to take the particularities of the destination into consideration. Characteristics such as the structure of tourism, the pace of tourism development, tourist behaviour, the condition of tourist and host relations, environmental, political, economic and social characteristics as well as the existing infrastructure play an important role and may influence the level of carrying capacity of a destination. In literature, three main components are distinguished which are interrelated and mutually influenced: the political-economic component, the socio-cultural component and the physical-environmental component. (Coccossis, Mexa, 2004, in Coccossis, 2004, 58f) The creation of workplaces in traditional industries in rural areas would fall into the field of economic effects, but at the same time also influences the social component. Therefore, a holistic point of view is crucial when elaborating the carrying capacity of a destination.

The definition of tourism carrying capacity starts with the definition of goals, evaluative descriptions of accepted changes and descriptive elements presenting the system in terms of environmental, social, political and economic characteristics. Constraints, bottlenecks and impacts have to be pointed out. (Coccossis, Mexa, 2004, in Coccossis, 2004, 61-63) COCCOSIS proposes an outline of the process of evaluating the carrying capacity of a destination by describing eight steps as a guideline:

1. **Analysis of the system**, including the three components mentioned earlier, physical-ecological, socio-cultural and political-economic. Detailed knowledge of the area in question, along with relationships that exist with neighbouring areas, are important.
2. **Analysis of tourism development** requires a detailed market analysis on supply and demand, future trends and developments, type of tourists, tourist attractions and the particularities of the destination.
3. **Analysis of the implications of tourism development for each component**, referring to the analysis of impacts, driving forces and causes given the current development of the specific components.
4. **Impact assessment** deals again and more in detail with the impacts on the three key components such as conflicts, threats and risks.
5. **Definition of the tourism carrying capacity for each component** includes the evaluation of bottlenecks and restrictions of the physical-ecological, socio-cultural and political-economic component as well as the selection of appropriate indicators in order to express and measure the desires levels or thresholds.
6. **Elaboration of alternative tourism development options** and alternative courses of action considering the specified constraints which remain unchangeable.

7. **Definition of the total carrying capacity of the system.** The preferable option elaborated in step six serves in order to define the total carrying capacity of a destination.
8. **Implementation of the total carrying capacity** refers to the final definition of constraints and bottlenecks the preparation of a final list of indicators, standards and thresholds as well as the definition of policies and organisational measures in order to implement them.
9. **Monitoring** is crucial in order to ensure long-term viability of the concept. At this point a set of indicators can be applied in order to identify violations of carrying capacity limits and provide data for future development.

FENNELL (1999, 123) proposes an application of the concept of tourism carrying capacity in combination with the destination life cycle by BUTLER. In other words a re-conceptionalisation of the life cycle model as it was developed in the 1980s. The basic curve remains the same but in a much more flattened form that at no point surpasses the critical social and ecological capacity limit. Instead of the steep introduction phase of BUTLERS' model, a slowly but steadily rising curve passes the stages of exploration, involvement and development before reaching a plateau in the consolidation phase. This final level has to be situated between the economic minimum level and the social and ecological capacity limit.

The concept of tourism carrying capacity is highly discussed and not generally accepted. Criticism arises due to the subjectivity of certain aspects, the inexactness of data and results, and the problems when it comes to implementing carrying capacity limits. CLARK (2002, in Coccossis, 2004, 40) describes it as a theoretical model "[...] divorced from reality [...]" which provides little guidance for practical implementation and has to be seen as a "guiding framework and less as scientific and operational definitions" (Mexa, Coccossis, 2004, in Coccossis, 2004, 40) Furthermore, it seems quite unrealistic that damage would arise at a specific number of tourists coming to a place. As a response to the fact that tourism carrying capacity can not be measured by absolute values, the concepts of "limits of acceptable change" and "visitor impact management" (Glasson, Godfrey, Goodey 1995, 2) have emerged throughout the last few years. The former refers to the assessment of tourism impacts on the destination and the definition of limits for tolerated changes and the latter stands for a set of actions that manage and control the impacts of tourism.

Furthermore the concept of tourism capacity includes multi-dimensional and complex issues that can cause political problems by accepting growth limits. It has to be adapted for every destination as the characteristics encountered are never the same. Tourism carrying capacity "cannot provide the basis for some magic formula for estimating how much is too much." (Mexa, Coccossis, 2004, in Coccossis, 2004, 40) Nevertheless "carrying capacity is likely to become a central concern in tourism management." (Coccossis, 2004, in Coccossis, 2004, 10). The analysis of the appropriate tourism carrying capacity can avoid adverse effects and help to find solutions for sustainable development, especially for destinations with fragile components, such as small islands.

5.2.5 Indicators

Indicators are mainly quantitative measures that intend to indicate a specific situation and, in consequence, the evolution of the aspect in question. "An indicator is meant to indicate something beyond the property it expresses prima facie" (Mukherjee 1975, in Sirakay, Jamal, Choi, 2001, in Weaver, 2001, 415)

According to the OECD (1997, in Sirakay, Jamal, Choi, 2001, in Weaver, 2001, 415) indicators are "an empirical interpretation of reality and not reality itself. [...] The three major functions of indicators are: simplification, quantification, and communication." Good indicators should provide a basis for anticipative and preventive decision making for tourism planners and managers by indicating the actual level of development. "Indicators are, therefore, both a tool for managers today and an investment in the future. [...]" (WTO, 1996, 11)

In general, six types of technical indicators can be distinguished: direct indicators refer to a measure of the variable itself, whereas indirect indicators analyse an issue related to the actual variable in question; descriptive and analytical indicators give either qualitative or quantitative information; objective versus subjective indicators, the latter reflecting the comments and information given by people and the former counting the conduct and conditions in a given situation. (Sirakaya, Jamal, Choi, 2001, in Weaver, 2001, 415f)
Besides a core set of indicators, specific destination indicators can be defined in order to better respond to the particular needs for information. As they vary according to the particularities of the destination, their exact definition is crucial. The data has to be

available and preferably easily retrievable. The indicator has to be transparent and credible in order to make it understandable for the public. Indicators have to respond directly to the problem, allow comparison with other areas and show trends over time. The availability of thresholds and limits allows benchmarking and the analysis of overall trends in the industry. (WTO, 1996, 38-41) Furthermore, the number of indicators should be manageable and each should have a high degree of reliability and predictive capacity. (Sirakaya, Jamal, Choi, 2001, in Weaver, 2001, 419)

Indicators don't deliver ready to use data, hence the results require further interpretation. The results can not be said to be positive or negative instantly as it depends on the point of view of the different stakeholders. "The indicator shows change and signals potential for concern" (WTO, 1996, 25)
Indicators and benchmarking are relatively new tools in the field of sustainable development as they emerged throughout the 1990s. Their emphasis lies in measuring the progress towards sustainability. These are mainly economic factors, but also increasingly social and cultural issues. (Synergy 2000, 61) The development of sustainability indicators is in its infancy and differs from traditional indicators in the sense that they consider the "[...] complex interrelationships and interdependencies of resources and stakeholders in the tourism system." (Sirakaya, Jamal, Choi, 2001, in Weaver, 2001, 418) Indicators must influence policy and decision making on all levels and cover all components of sustainable development. Furthermore, it is recommended that community participation be enhanced in order to reflect the vision of the local population. (Sirakaya, Jamal, Choi, 2001, in Weaver, 2001, 419)

"The use of indicators as a way to identify and define TCC limits is a simple and more flexible approach" in comparison with the process described previously and can also enable managers to confront data in the short and medium term in order to identify increased pressure caused by tourism. (Coccossis, Mexa, 2004, in Coccossis, 2004, 70) Mc ELROY and ALBUQUERQUE (1998, in Coccossis, 2004, 70) propose a *Tourism Penetration Index* made up of three indicators: "visitor spending per capita, average density per 1000 population and number of hotels per km^2". This index considers the economic component by evaluating the tourism spending that falls on each resident, social issues regarding the proportion of tourists and local population, as well as the physical component with regards to the density of tourism beds in the destination. Nevertheless, it is a very basic set of key indicators which can only serve as a benchmark with other destinations or illustrate evolution over time.

The concept of indicators can be applied to single businesses just as to entire destinations. It is a methodological approach, hence it is characterised by a high level of transparency. Benchmarking with indicators not only allows comparing businesses or destinations among each other but also their progress from year to year, hence continuous performance improvement can be measured easily. Due to the technical data required, difficulties may arise for smaller businesses and third party verification is difficult. (Synergy, 2000, 61) Other obstacles in the work with indicators include: limited data availability and little data comparability. (Kaae, 2001, in Mc Cool, 2001, 293)

The process of developing indicators has to be based on a well defined and shared vision of the sustainability goals. The scope of indicators has to be decided on, considering the spatial, temporal and political framework. Furthermore, an indicator framework has to be defined. In literature, several types are discussed such as the "domain-based", "goal based" or "sectoral" framework. (Waldron, Williams, 2002, in Harris, Griffin, Williams, 2002, 182f)

Once the basics are defined, the indicators have to be well defined according to the goals or the problems identified. Indicators are multidisciplinary, they can not be considered as an isolated, self explanatory figure but only in a broader context of mutual influence. COCCOSSIS and MEXA (2004, in Coccossis, 2004, 87-89) propose a list of socio-cultural indicators which is not exhaustive, but can be considered as a suggestion.

1. Demographic
   Population growth rate, age structure
   Population density (persons/km2)

2. Tourist flow
   Number of tourists per host population
   Number of beds, places and overnight stays
   Number of arrivals per 100 inhabitants
   Number of tourists per area unit of the destination
   Number of tourists per density area
   Number of tourists per month (seasonality)

3. Employment
    Decrease in employment in traditional activities
    Number of part-time and full time employment
    Number of tourist beds per local people employed
    Migrant labour compared to local people employed in tourism

4. Social behaviour
    Percentage of tourists understanding the language of destination
    Number of mixed couples compared to the national average
    Rate of premature school leavers

5. Health and safety
    Crime level
    Average aid emergencies during the tourist season compared to the annual average
    Number of crimes against tourists

6. Psychological issues
    Rate of tourists satisfied with their vacation
    Rate of local population satisfied with tourism development
    Number of local establishments open all year round compared to the total number of tourism businesses
    Number of complaints by tourists and hosts
    Rate of residents directly and indirectly benefiting from tourism
    Displacement of members of local population due to tourism development

The European initiative VISIT set up a set of sustainability indicators to create an outline for tourism planners. According to this list, the percentage of land owned by non-residents and the involvement of stakeholders' ratio have to be added. (VISIT, 2004)

Indicators can be used as a management and decision making tool, but mainly they are applied for monitoring tourism impacts. The objective is to "track changes in social, natural, cultural, economic and political areas". (Sirakaya, Jamal, Choi, 2001, in Weaver, 2001, 413) No matter what indicators are finally used for, results require further interpretation and have to be reported in forms adapted to the reader.

5.2.6 Destination management tools

The variety of tools to manage and control negative impacts caused by tourism is ample. Managers usually modify the marketing mix in order to increase the demand. Visitor management is an even broader concept, including quantitative as well as qualitative measures such as access regulation, managing visitor numbers by group size or by visitor type, regulating visitor behaviour, regulating the equipment to be used and activities, changing the site itself as well as its facilities, providing interpretation and education programs etc. (Page, Dowling, 2002, 230)

Pricing

The most commonly applied tools are pricing measures based on the price-demand curve. In oversaturated tourism destinations or during high season, high entrance fees or exaggerated prices are introduced in order to discourage people and lower the number of tourism arrivals. Critics of this approach state that it can be seen as ethically incorrect. A less radical approach of pricing would be to use tourist taxes for environmental protection or social development programs. (Swarbrooke, 2004, 31)

De-marketing

De-marketing is another tool used to reduce visitor numbers, using the marketing mix to discourage rather than to attract tourists. For example, through the reduction of promotional material, the demand can be lowered. These measures will initiate conflicts and protests within the community and it has to be assured beforehand that the problem merits such drastic measures. A different approach of visitor management is to lead tourist flows from honey-pot destinations to either less developed tourist areas or to low seasons by increasing promotional efforts and by creating new tourism products. (Swarbrooke, 2004, 29f)

Zoning

Zoning and clustering are two concepts applied for the regulation of environmental impacts, but they also have implications in social and cultural matters. Zoning refers to the creation of zones within an area which require different management measures or protection levels. Especially in areas of nature preservation and national parks, this approach is widely used. The concept of clustering also refers to the creation of tourist ghettos within an area, the "concentration of tourist attractions and facilities in specified areas" (Inskeep, 1988, in Page, Dowling, 2002, 231). The idea is the creation of zones only for tourism use in order to provide infrastructure and other facilities in a more efficient ways and to avoid the dispersion of tourism. These tourist areas should be situated where no other economic activities are realised and were the development doesn't harm the environment or local community. GUNN (1994, in Page, Dowling, 2002, 231) suggested clustering for large scale tourism destinations as it allows more control of the development of tourism. (Page, Dowling, 2002, 229–231)

5.2.7 Education and guidelines

A qualitative management approach is supposed to guide the visitors' behaviour towards a positive and less harming conduct with respect to the environment and the local community. Education and appropriate information play an important role in enhancing the acceptance of the local population of tourism. These factors play an important role and improve the intercultural exchange between visitors and visited. Respect for other cultures is a key factor when travelling. A lack of this basic acceptance of cultural differences impedes any intercultural relationships and destroys any possibility for mutual learning and understanding. Information can reduce prejudices, rectify wrong expectations and prevent the creation of stereotypes. KAAE (2001, in Mc Cool, 2001, 292) argues that "another way of reducing impacts is by changing the behaviour of tour operators and tourists through the use of codes of conduct".

These kinds of guidelines exist on different levels, addressing different stakeholders or referring to diverse issues and can be distinguished as below: (Gortázar, Marín, 1999, 79)
- Codes of the tourism industry in general
- Codes that are concerned with specific sectors or activities

- Codes about the behaviour of tourists
- Codes addressing the local population of the destination

Especially in the field of Ecotourism, the use of codes of conduct is popular and very promising in order to enhance ecological awareness and appropriate behaviour. Social guidelines (also called visitor codes, visitor guidelines or codes of conduct) were first developed in the late 1970s and early 1980s. They can provide important information to tourists concerning the appropriate conduct in a given area. The main objective is the change of visitors' behaviour and as a consequence the reduction of environmental, social and cultural impacts of tourism. (Synergy, 2000, 57)

A rather general code of conduct can include hints for the election of an appropriate tour operator, for contracting local businesses and about environmental aspects. Information regarding the culture and which activities could cause disturbance in the area and how to behave during the stay should be included. (Gortázar, Marín, 1999, 81) A code of conduct can prevent unpleasant situations, especially when the cultural differences between the visited and visitors' culture are evident. According to BLANGY and EPLER WOOD (1992, in Wearing, 2001, in Weaver, 2001, 405) well-formulated social guidelines, incorporated in an overall strategy, can enhance desirable and acceptable behaviour with respect to the following areas:

1. Local customs and traditions
2. Permission for photographs
3. Dress codes
4. Language
5. Invasion of privacy
6. Response to begging
7. Use and abuse of technological gadgetry
8. Bartering and bargaining
9. Indigenous rights
10. Local officials
11. Off-limit areas

Codes of conduct have a series of strengths: the rise of awareness, general applicability to all sectors and industries, flexibility, modification according to types of tourism and environment. (Synergy, 2000, 57)

Social guidelines have to be formulated specifically for every destination as it is necessary that they reflect precisely the local culture, values and customs. Their transmission should, in the best case, be executed by all stakeholders, reaching from public organisations, tourist boards, to associations in the industry and local people. Everybody can play a role in the education of tourists about environmental, cultural and social issues. The integration of local people in the education process requires pre-information and education in order to make them aware of their responsibilities and rights. (Wearing, 2001, in Weaver, 2001, 404f)

Not only visitors' education should be considered for impact management but equally the training and education of people directly or indirectly involved in tourism. "Developing the right tools to involve and assist people in improving quality, in line with agreed standards [...]" (European Commission, 1999, 50) is the main challenge. Cooperation within the tourism industry is crucial to ensure efficient training, education and exchange of information. The creation of networks is a good option to establish working groups to discuss certain issues and propose solutions. The training has to be offered either free of charge or at a reduced cost, and interesting topics have to be treated in order to attract people.

5.3 Controlling and Monitoring

Monitoring and controlling are key factors in any strategic planning process and decide upon the success or failure of management strategies. Without effective monitoring, no information is available on the progress made or not made. Efficient monitoring has to be carried out systematically, continuously and periodically at predetermined moments. (Eagles, Mc Cool, Haynes, 2002, 151) It has to be initiated at a very early phase, such as the decision making and the definition of strategies stages, and continue or even be enhanced throughout the implementation phase. Results obtained by monitoring have to be used as feedback in order to evaluate the effectiveness of measures taken, future trends and to decide on further strategies.

Two different approaches can be identified for monitoring of tourism. Firstly, the monitoring of visitor impacts, which is realised by periodic measurement according to predefined indicators regarding economic, environmental, social and cultural impacts. The second approach is the monitoring of service quality, which refers to the quality intended to be provided for visitors as well as the quality perceived by tourists. A third component has to be added, regarding the satisfaction of the local community with the development of tourism. (Eagles, Mc Cool, Haynes, 151)

Monitoring programs need to be well planned in order to be effective and bring about the desired results. It should be integrated in the general planning and management of a destination. The obtained results have to be taken into consideration for decision taking on all organisational levels.

Monitoring with indicators is the most commonly used approach. Also, social auditing is another tool used to monitor the well being of a society. It comprises a "[…] systematic, documented, periodic and objective evaluation of how well social organisation, management and equipment are performing with the aim of helping to safeguard the culture and community […]." (Synergy, 2000)

Conclusion

The planning process is *the* key factor for successful implementation and carrying out of measures for sustainable development. The appropriate timing of planning is essential. In other words, planning has to be completed in advance in order to act, instead of react, on negative consequences. Planning shall not be confused with crisis management and therefore, shall focus on long-term measures.

Several concepts of managing impacts were discussed and a theoretical overview was provided. The tourism management spectrum proposes a very general categorisation of actions to be taken. The concept of TCC is very theoretic and complex. It is complicated to be carried out and limitation of tourist growth in general provokes criticism and objection. Nevertheless, a further step in the evolution of carrying capacities is the definition of limits of acceptable change which focus more on the qualitative evaluation of limits for further development. The establishment of a set of indicators can serve as a basis for decision making, controlling and especially for benchmarking. Indicators are very flexible and can easily be adapted to specific situations. The marketing mix is used to regulate tourist flows in a destination. Usually, prices are lowered in order to attract more tourists. In the case of regulation for a sustainable development, the contrary happens; by increasing the price level, tourists are discouraged to visit the destination. The different approaches are not mutually exclusive, but on the contrary may complement one another. The best choice is therefore a mix of concepts implemented at the same time or during different planning phases, according to the specific situation.

6 LA GOMERA

La Gomera is the second smallest of the seven Canary Islands, situated west of the major island Tenerife. At the closest point, the distance between the two islands is about 30 km. La Gomera has a very characteristic circular shape and its surface counts 369km^2. Its volcanic origin and the long lasting erosion process it has undergone have given the island its characteristics, spectacular ravines, costal cliffs and impressive peaks, such as the highest peak *Garajonay* that rises 1,487m above sea level. The National Park, Garajonay, which was declared UNESCO world heritage site in 1981 in order to protect the unique laurel forest, covers about 11% of the island. (Ladrón de Guevara, 2004, 6)

The island is characterised by a great climatic variety. The northern part (Hermigua, Agulo, Vallehermoso) shows a stable climate, mild temperatures and a medium degree of humidity that creates perfect conditions for agriculture. The south of the island, on the contrary, has higher temperatures, less humidity and scarce vegetation. The southern municipalities (San Sebastián, Alajeró, Valle Gran Rey) are now the most densely populated of the island and are most developed in terms of tourism. (Ladrón de Guevara, 2004, 7)

Traditionally speaking, the economy of La Gomera was based on agriculture and the island was, until recent times, self-sufficient; importation of goods was not necessary. The more fertile north was historically the more densely populated and wealthier part. "Immigration and declining agriculture meant a substantial drop in population [...]", which caused severe economic difficulties. Due to the migration flows, numerous houses, especially in the rural areas of the island, have been abandoned. Recently some of these houses have been revitalised and converted into rural houses used as second homes or accommodation for tourism. (Ladrón de Guevara, 2004, 14)

La Gomera shows a very low population density, the total population of 19,580 is mainly concentrated in the southern municipalities, San Sebastian, Alajero and Valle Gran Rey. 67% of the population live in the south, whereas 33% live in the north (ISTAC, 2004, 13). The average population density of La Gomera is 52.9 habitants per square kilometre.

Cultural resources and the social development of the island are highly influenced by its history. The island was already known in antique times and populated by a tribe called *Guanches* that had arrived from north western Africa about 1000 b.c. (Hernández Hernández, 2000, 104) The island entered western history in the 15th century with the arrival of European conquerors. The following centuries were marked by revolutions of the local population, which ended in slavery and violent battles. A historic event which is promoted, especially in tourism, is the stay of Christopher Columbus on La Gomera in 1492 before he left to discover America. (Patronato de Turismo, 2005) Other factors that influenced La Gomeras' culture were geographic isolation until the 1970s and the emigration of important parts of the population to South America, especially to Cuba and Venezuela. During the last decade, a certain number of descendants of these emigrants has returned.

6.1 Rural Tourism on the Canary Islands

Rural tourism is estimated to continue growing on international level. According to the World Research Institute (2000, in Ecotural, 2004, 27) an estimated growth rate of 20% annually is to be expected. Nevertheless, it will remain a niche sector as massive changes in demand towards rural tourism are not aspired anymore. (Ecotural, 2004, 27f)
La Gomera is situated in one of the most important tourism destinations in the world. The Canary Islands have experienced a spectacular boom in tourism since the 1970s. (CES, 2003, 108)

Rural tourism is not only developing on La Gomera, but increasingly on all the Canary Islands. Tourism in island regions shows very specific characteristics and many negative examples are known of massified, crowded and concrete-covered island destinations. Many of these areas in the European Union are characterised by accommodation densities that vary between 75 and 150 beds per square kilometre. These figures even exceed the population densities of densely populated areas on the continent. In total, islands in the European Union receive about four billion tourists per year. (Insula, 2005) The Canary Islands are only one example of island destinations with massive tourism. The tourist arrivals on the Canary Islands count around 15 millions per year and the total bed capacity is close to 500,000 beds. (ISTAC, 2004, 22) "A lack of integration of the tourist industry in the natural, cultural and human environment can easily upset the fragile balance that characterises island tourist resorts, making them economically and ecologically vulnerable." (Insula, 2005)

The sustainable development of island regions also forms an essential part of the Agenda 21 (Rio de Janeiro 1992), where chapter 17 explicitly points out the special situation of islands in all terms: environmental, economic and social. "Their small size, limited resources, geographical dispersion and their isolation all put them at a disadvantage." (Insula, 2005) Rural Tourism is a form of tourism that goes hand in hand with sustainable development of tourism and islands.

For that reason, the promotion and development of tourism on the Canary Islands has focused on rural tourism. The organisation ACANTUR is actively promoting this form of tourism on the Canary Islands. Whereas the islands La Gomera, La Palma and El Hierro are known as rural tourism destinations and are actively promoted as such, the major islands also have been focusing more and more on alternative forms of tourism. The numbers of rural accommodation facilities is increasing constantly on all Canary Islands: at the beginning of 2004 a total of 626 rural accommodations were registered. (ISTAC, 2005) La Gomera forms part of this highly saturated mass tourism destination, but intends to be different in terms of tourism development.

6.2 Development of tourism on La Gomera

Tourism development on La Gomera has so far been different to the development of the major Canary Islands. Thanks to its relatively isolated situation until the 1970s, La Gomera has been saved from mass tourism and the construction boom that still characterises its' neighbour island Tenerife. The development of tourism on La Gomera can be divided into three phases which are defined by important events for the island. The first period was when tourism was non existent and when La Gomera was not regularly connected by ferry with its major neighbouring island, Tenerife. The start of a regular ferry line initialised the development of tourism on the island which started slowly and in an unorganised way. With the association of rural tourism, another phase emerged: the development of a more sustainable form of tourism.

Period of geographic isolation

The connection between Tenerife and La Gomera was very limited until 1974. Before 1974, the ferry company Transmediterránea provided transport between the two islands by ferry only twice weekly. During this period, tourism was practically non-existent. The demographic situation of La Gomera was characterised by a high level of emigration. This emigration was a two phase phenomenon: the first wave of Gomerans left at the beginning of the 20th century to Cuba and the second wave was from the 1940s until the 1960s to Venezuela and Tenerife. (Reyes Aguilar, 2002, 75f) As illustrated in the figure below, La Gomera lost nearly half of its population and only at the beginning of the 1980s did the population start to grow slightly. In 2003, La Gomera counted 19,580 inhabitants. (ISTAC 2004, 6)

Due to the depopulation of the island during the 1960s and 1970s, the development of tourism was hardly possible as no infrastructure was available. An even bigger problem was that no restructure of the traditional agriculture was carried out so that the island, traditionally based on the primary sector, lost its economic basis and suffered severe problems. (Reyes Aguilar, 2002, 80)

The figure below illustrates the population increase on La Gomera in the second half of the 19th century until the 1950s, thanks to moderate economic growth. Until the 1970s, nearly half of the population emigrated and since the 1980s the population has increased again due to migration flows. La Gomera has changed from a sending to a receiving region.

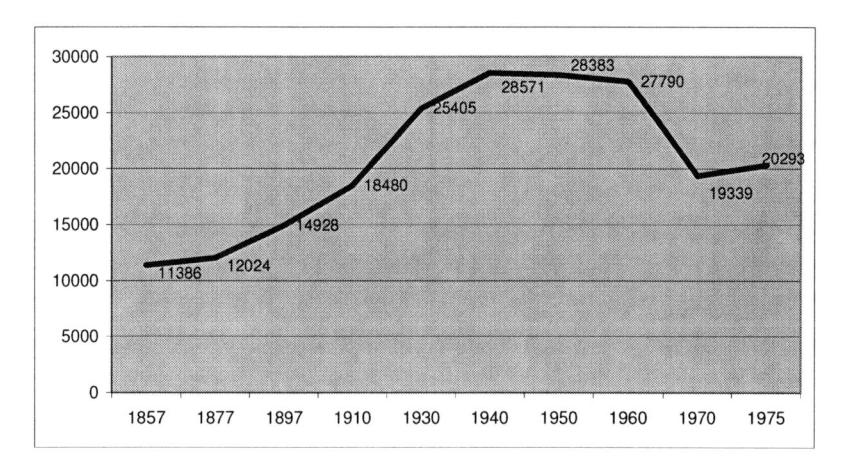

Figure 15: Population of La Gomera[17]

The population development of the Canary Islands in general is quite interesting. Until the 1960s, the Canary Islands were affected by a high level of emigration, whereas the situation has changed since the beginning of the 1970s when a flow of immigration emerged towards the islands. The level of population growth due to immigration was estimated to be 9.9% per year from 1991-1995 and 16.9 per year for the period 1996-2000. Between 1976 and 2002, the active population of the Canary Islands as a whole increased by 72%. (CES, 2003, 298) This phenomenon was more or less marked on each of the Canary Islands and caused severe economic, social and cultural problems.

Year	Migration
1941-50	-22,000
1951-60	-35,000
1961-70	-52,000
1971-80	68,000
1981-90	25,000

Table 3: Migration flow of Canary Islands[18]

---

[17] after Reyes Aguilar (2002), 58-62
[18] Centro de la cultura popular Canaria (1995), 33

1970s until today

At the beginning of the 1970s, additional communication was provided between Tenerife and La Gomera. From that moment on the island appeared on the tourist map. Still, no mass tourism could develop thanks to a lack of infrastructure and for this reason explicitly, individual tourists, hippies and hiking tourists were attracted. Tourism numbers still remained rather limited: 20,000 tourists visited La Gomera in 1973. (Nau, 1997, 36)

The end of isolation signed also the decline of agriculture on La Gomera. Products could be imported at lower prices than the local products cost and people were no more dependent on their own production. The smaller sized properties in difficult, exposed locations (terraced, steep land) and that had high opportunity costs, high exit barriers, high production costs, low economic qualification and strong external competition were the main factors disfavouring the primary sector activities. (Centro de la cultura popular Canaria, 1995, 68)

The development of tourism on La Gomera was very spontaneous, on a small-scale and demand driven. The existing demand created the offer which at the beginning was based on private initiatives. Fishermen in Valle Gran Rey for example, started to use their fishing boats to take tourists for a trip around the island. (Macleod, 2003, in Hall, 2003, 196) The situation nowadays has changed, but there is little initiative from the population of La Gomera to participate in structured and planned tourism development. Important parts of the tourism offer on the island belong to foreigners and the multinational company Fred Olsen that owns a large part of the tourism infrastructure in Playa Santiago and land in the southern part.

Until the 1980s, going to La Gomera was an insider tip for globetrotters and individual tourists. Since then mostly Germans have discovered the island. From 1970 until 1990, the accommodation offered increased by about 500% in only twenty years and further increase is planned. (Nau, 1997, 36) Conventional tourism infrastructure is beginning to be built, especially in the areas of Valle Gran Rey and Playa Santiago and this is forcing back small scale, private accommodation in order to enhance quality and attract more financially sound tourists. Macleod (2003, in Hall, 2003, 198) confirms this development: "the profile of visitors is changing, favouring those taking package holidays [...]" the spontaneous development of ecotourism is becoming more professional and competitive.

Two important issues characterise the development of tourism on La Gomera: the increasing market power of the multinational company Fred Olsen and the popularity as a destination for day-trips from Tenerife.

As stated on the Website of Fred Olsen Lines, the business activities currently include "the passengers and cargo transport in regular maritime lines, the hotel business, restoration and cultural leisure". (Fred Olsen, 2005) In other words, the Fred Olsen group has a strong position in tourism, especially in the field of transport, and provides various tourism services on La Gomera in terms of a vertical integration; different types of accommodation, restaurants and a golf course.

Due to its proximity to Tenerife, La Gomera is a day-tripping destination for tourists spending their holidays on the larger neighbouring island. All-inclusive products are offered by tour operators on Tenerife. This form of tourism has only small economic repercussions on La Gomera as all services are paid in advance and during the trip hardly any expenses are necessary.

Rural tourism development

Rural tourism already appeared during the first period of tourism development on La Gomera, characterised by a slow growth rate and small scale. Firstly, rural tourism developed in the north part of La Gomera was based on private initiatives where old houses in rural areas were revitalised to be used as tourist accommodation and to substitute declining agricultural incomes. Only during the 1990s did the name and distinction of rural tourism appear when in 1994 the C.I.T. (centre of initiatives for rural development in the north of La Gomera) was founded in order to organise and promote the offer of rural tourism. Also at that time, public subsidies were provided to facilitate the rehabilitation of traditional buildings. Since then the number of rural houses has increased and projects are carried out in order to continuously improve the environmental and service quality of the offer.

The offer of rural accommodation increased by 65.7% between 2001 and 2003. A total of 58 legalised rural houses made up the offer in 2003. As illustrated in the figure below, the offer is concentrated in the municipality of Hermigua (43.10%). The northern part of the island provides 79.3% of the total offer of rural houses on La Gomera. This is due to the concentration of rural development in the north and the earlier association of proprietors of rural houses in this area.

Municipalities	Rural houses	% of total	n° of beds	% of total
Agulo	13	22.41	82	27.70
Hermigua	25	43.10	125	42.23
Vallehermoso	8	13.79	37	12.50
San Sebastian	6	10.34	26	8.78
Alajero	3	5.17	11	3.72
Valle Gran Rey	3	5.17	15	5.07
TOTAL	58	100	296	100

Table 4: Offer of rural tourism accommodation on La Gomera 2003[19]

There is a high level of illegal offers on La Gomera, referring to tourist accommodation promoted as rural houses but not officially registered as such. According to estimates made within the scope of the market study of rural tourism on La Gomera (Ecotural, 2004, 42) only 60.13% of the houses are legalised, the rest of 39.87% are illegal or in the course of legalisation.

The offer of rural accommodation has to be furthermore distinguished, in rural houses and rural hotels which both have to meet certain standards regarding the age, the architectural style and the location. Construction has to have a patrimonial and ethnographical value and has to at least date back to the 1950s. Furthermore, specific regulations exist regarding the renovation of a rural house and its adoption for tourism. In the paragraph §618 of the PTE development plan, the regulations for rural tourism are stipulated and the territory of La Gomera is divided in various zones of future tourism development. (Cabildo de La Gomera, PTE)

The following table gives an indication on the importance of rural tourism on La Gomera by evaluating population density as well as the density of rural tourism. With a benchmark of the Canary Islands, La Gomera shows a very low population density with only 52.95 people per km^2 in comparison with 254.45 as an average of the Canary Islands. Hermigua shows 6.91 beds per km^2 and 12.64 beds per 100 habitants at the highest concentration of rural tourism.

---

[19] after Consejería de Turismo (2005)

Municipalities	Population	Km²	hab/km²	Beds	Bed/km²	Bed/100 hab
Agulo	1,189	25.39	46.83	128	5.04	10.77
Hermigua	2,167	39.67	54.63	274	6.91	12.64
Vallehermoso	3,109	109.32	28.44	152	1.39	4.89
San Sebastian	6,902	113.59	60.76	112	0.99	1.62
Alajero	1,726	49.42	34.93	40	0.81	2.32
Valle Gran Rey	4,487	32.36	138.66	109	3.37	2.43
La Gomera	**19,580**	**369.75**	**52.95**	**815**	**2.20**	**4.16**
Canarias	1,894,868	7447	254.45			

Table 5: Rural accommodation offer and population density on 1st of January 2003[20]

Considering the general tourism offer of La Gomera, the percentage of rural tourism increased in 2001, rural tourism establishments represented 1.73% of the total offer and rural beds 2.10%. In 2003, the percentage of beds in rural accommodation was already 3.81%, non-hotels (apartments and pensions) made up for 63.64% and hotels 23.66% of the total of beds. (Ecotural, 2004, 46)

According to the development plan PTE, in which the future development of tourism is defined for La Gomera, rural tourism will grow up to 12.8% of the total tourism offer by 2013. The total number of tourist beds will therefore reach 16,987, which means an increase of about 150% (6,783 beds in 2003). (Ecotural, 2004, 47)

Conclusion

Future development of tourism on La Gomera is not yet planned and decided on. No general legal tourism plan, but only guidelines and previsions, exist. This situation leads to uncontrolled, inconsequential and disorganised development. Voices afraid of La Gomera becoming a "little Tenerife" (Nau, 1997, 36) become loud. The president of the island's government (Ideatur, 2002, 6) declared that tourism on La Gomera is, however, still in its infancy, so the challenges to come can be planned and well considered. The objective has to be set on the creation of a balance between the preservation of a unique environment and the enhancement of the living standard of the local population. Furthermore, the demand of high quality tourism has to be satisfied. The president suggested that the desired development for La Gomera should be focused on rural tourism and restricted development of conventional tourism.

---

[20] Ecotural (2004), 44

6.3 Resource diagnosis

"It should be recognised that all types of new development bring impacts [...]" on a community. (WTO, 2001, 127) Tourism is usually only one factor influencing local development, others such as modern media, television, internet and migration are only examples which are playing a role for the development on for La Gomera. (WTO, 1993, 111) Tourism resources have the capability to attract visitors to a specific area and different types of such resources have to be distinguished, for example between the natural, cultural and artificial attractions. (Organismo Autónomo de Parques Nacionales, 2005, 1f)

Social diagnosis

Most of La Gomeras' attractions and its atmosphere are based on the socio-historic development of the island; Historical development is based on the aboriginal habitants, the *Guanches*, the European conquerors of the 15th century, the economic development and long lasting geographic isolation and the emigration and decline of agriculture in the 19th century.

According to the experts interviewed within the scope of the questionnaire on social and cultural aspects on La Gomera, the most important social issues on La Gomera today are the high unemployment rate, alcoholism, drug addiction, machismo, the status of women, the low motivation of the population, little participation and interest in decision-making, the low level of professional education, the high level of failure in school, the loss of rural culture as a base for living, low funds for socially disfavoured groups and a lack of cooperation among development agents. (Expert questionnaire, 2005)

A severe demographic problem is the aging of the population of La Gomera. In 1960, more than 50% of the population was less than 25 years old. Today the situation has changed and in 2001 only about 30% were below that age. (ISTAC, 2004, 7) Until the 1960s, the Canary Islands were characterised by a young demographic structure, but throughout the 1980s and 1990s the demographic pyramid showed an increasing aging of the population.

There are various factors influencing the social situation on La Gomera, primarily the ongoing change of the economic system from a primary sector to a tertiary sector based economy. Furthermore, the geographically unbalanced development of tourism (north-south) as well as the concentration on only one economic sector, create negative social impacts. Also the limited distance and enhanced mobility of people, emigration, as well a new technology (internet and TV, for example) are responsible for changes in the social system of La Gomera. (Expert Questionnaire, 2005)

Social aspects can not be considered as tourism attractions but they build the basis for a tourism friendly atmosphere that is crucial for the development of tourism in a destination. Most of the tourism resources such as cultural elements, traditions, monuments and the landscape are based on the local society and its evolution throughout history.

Cultural Resources

"In many places, cultural traditions are being lost because of the influences of modern development generally. Tourism can be an important vehicle for revitalising and conserving, [...]" (WTO, 2001, 85) Furthermore, it is said that tourism can enhance the self-esteem of the local population, as well as increasing their pride for their culture. Administration, and also the local population, become more aware of the importance of cultural development and might take action against cultural loss.

Gomeran experts were asked about the importance, that the local population attributes to their culture. They are of the opinion that the level of importance is still relatively low and in some cases people are not conscious of the importance of cultural values, traditions and cultural elements. Nevertheless, others think that people are beginning to realise culture has to be preserved, transmitted and lived. The participation level in cultural activities depends on the type of cultural elements; cultural events are more popular than craftwork and other elements of material culture. The situation with respect to the young generation is generally seen in a very negative way and some experts believe that certain cultural elements will be lost with the next generation. (Expert questionnaire, 2005)

The cultural elements that create the Gomeran identity and are considered to be the most characteristic, distinguishing La Gomera from other Canary Islands are defined by the experts as the following:

Cultural Element	Description
Rural culture / Agriculture, farming	
El Silbo	Unique pre-Hispanic whistle language used to communicate across long distances. (Ladrón de Guevara, 2004, 12)
Miel de Palma	Liquid, dark honey from the palm tree.
Patches	Due to the steep slopes people were forced to terrace the land in order to cultivate vegetables, corn, potatoes, plantains etc. the rural landscape of the island is highly modified and characterised by these patches
Network of footpaths	The traditionally used footpaths are still in use, today mainly by hiking tourists. They build a network covering the entire island in order to reach also the most isolated settlements
Folklore	
Musical instruments	Las *chácaras* are a type of castanets but bigger and *el tambor* a sort of drum played with sticks. Those are said to be the essence of the soul of the island, as they accompanied the oral transmission of La Gomeran history. (Perera, 2001, 70)
El Baile del tambor	A dance presented at religious celebrations, accompanied by the music of the "tambor" and songs with several verses. (Perera, 2001, 16)
El romancero gomero	A musical poem in various strophes orally transmitted and continuously amplified.
The traditional dressing	
Fiestas and legends	
Most of the traditional festivities are based on religious celebrations and saints. Traditionally those celebrations constituted an occasion to meet people from the village or from other areas of the island. The calendar of festivities is especially full during summer. "Religion seems to have more cultural than spiritual importance on La Gomera". (Expert Questionnaire, 2005)	
Legends such as *Gara y Jonay* that gave the National park its name, *Las brujas de la Laguna Grande* and so on.	
Craftwork / Artisans	
Ceramic, rag rugs, wood and clay works, wickerwork, leatherworks and craftwork with palm leaves	
Gastronomy	
Almogrote	A cheese and oil dip with red pepper
Mojos	A variety of sauces on oil basis with different herbs and spices
Gofio	Traditionally, semolina of maize which is used as a

	complement to soups and deserts
Cress soup, different sweet dishes, cheese and vines	
Architecture	
Traditional architecture shows varieties in urban or rural housing, farm houses, ovens, and the different periods. The traditional rural house was built of stone.	

Table 6: Cultural elements of La Gomera[21]

Most of the mentioned cultural elements date back to the population of the last two centuries, the European period of the island. But there are artefacts of pre-Hispanic times which form an important part of the historic culture of the island. Nevertheless, not much attention has been attributed so far to archaeological sites; most of them are not located, not excavated, in abandoned conditions or not accessible. (Organismo Autónomo de Parques Nacionales, 2005, 26)

All experts questioned agreed that most of those cultural elements linked to agriculture, farming and the rural lifestyle are in danger of extinction. As a pointed illustration we can look at the example of craftwork, which only 50 years ago was used on a daily basis in the households. Nowadays nobody uses wooden pots or plates so that products are now used only for decorative purposes. Folklore and elements historically passed on from mouth to mouth are in strong competition with modern technology, such as TV and internet. (Expert questionnaire, 2005)

La Gomera offers a wide range of cultural attractions. It has not only built monuments, but also it has its own specific rural culture and respective life style. It is impossible and not the this paper's objective to transmit an ample concept such as a culture to tourists staying for a holiday period. Nevertheless a lived-in culture is communicated more naturally and tourists can obtain an impression of authentic elements. It is therefore important to preserve cultural life and the cultural construction as a whole and not to isolate specific elements which are appropriate for commercialisation. Such elements would lose their authenticity and as a consequence, their attraction for the local population as well as for hosts.

---

[21] after Expert Questionnaire (2005)

Natural Resources

La Gomera offers a wide range of natural resources that are considered to be one of the main attractions for tourism. Until now many of its natural resources have been preserved thanks to the declaration of the central part of the island as UNESCO world heritage site and the installation of the national park.

Climate

The Climate is one primary natural resource favouring the development of tourism on La Gomera. A differentiation has to be made between the southern part with temperatures between 28° and 29° in summer and the north with an average of 25° during the same period. (Nau, 1997, 17) A moderate climate with little difference between summer and winter characterises the climate on the Canary Islands. The specific climate situation, with variations between the coastal zone in the south and the mountainous areas in the centre, creates a special atmosphere and attractiveness. Furthermore, the differing climatic areas are suitable for different types of activities.

Landscape

La Gomera is characterised by its spectacular landscape. Most of the characteristic elements exist due to the geological development of the volcanic islands and the erosion process. Ravines, fertile valleys, rock formations, cliffs and waterfalls are some examples characterising the natural landscape of La Gomera. Particularities of the cultural landscape are: the steep, terraced slopes for cultivation, the valleys in the north with plantain plantations and the "caseríos", small settlements in the mountain areas. Also fauna and flora form a characteristic part of the landscape. As to the flora of the island, essential differences exist between the climate zones: very dry in the south and humid in the north. La Gomera is an interesting destination especially for ornithologists and research on reptiles.

National Park Garajonay

The National Park Garajonay is situated in the centre of the island surrounding the highest peak, the *Alta de Garajonay* which ascends to 1,487m above sea level. It covers 11% of the islands surface and was declared a UNESCO world heritage site thanks to its unique laurel forest. (Ladrón de Guevara, 2004, 6) The National Park administration maintains a network of hiking-paths, lookout points and a visitor's centre. It constitutes one of the major tourist attractions on the island and combines natural, cultural and artificial attractions.

6.4 Set of sustainability indicators

Hardly any tourism research has been conducted on La Gomera so far and not much data is available. Figures elaborated by the ISTAC (statistic institute of the Canary Islands) and the government of the Canary Islands provide information on all islands, and some information is available from the insular authorities of La Gomera and the harbour authorities. Information about the rural tourism sector is available to a certain degree thanks to a market study conducted by the association of rural tourism Ecotural Gomera.

The following indicators were selected in order to reflect a developmental process towards more social and cultural sustainability. The indicator set is based on the assumption (also confirmed by the experts interviewed), that a socially and culturally sustainable tourism development on La Gomera is only possible within the framework of rural tourism. (Expert questionnaire, 2005)

6.4.1 General tourism indicators

Seasonality

Due to the mild and consistent climate of the Canary Islands, rural tourism is not affected by summer–winter seasonality. On the contrary, many foreign tourists choose it as a destination for escaping strong European winters and national tourists as a short trip destination. Nevertheless tourism arrivals show certain peaks during specific periods.

La Gomera

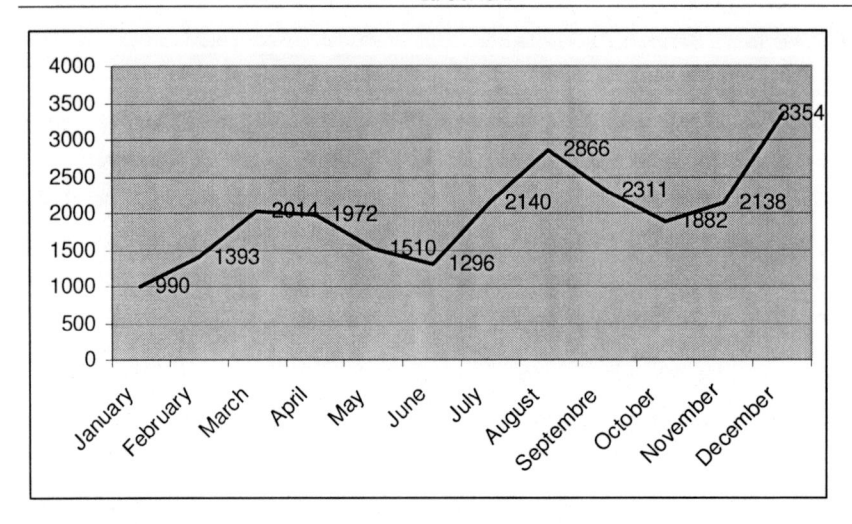

```
4000
3500                                                              3354
3000                                    2866
2500                                          2311
2000        2014 1972           2140                2138
1500    1393         1510                      1882
1000  990                1296
 500
   0
     January February March April May June July August September October November December
```

Figure 16: Rural tourist arrivals 2003 in Canary Islands[22]

The figures illustrated in the figure above represent an estimation of tourist arrivals for rural tourism for all Canary Islands. The seasonal variations can be considered to be similar on La Gomera.

Tourist arrivals

According to the harbour authorities of La Gomera, 650,794 passengers entered the island in 2003 by ferry from Tenerife. (Harbour authorities, 2004) As there are no official numbers of tourist arrivals available, only estimates can be made according to the passenger numbers published by the harbour authorities. The airport of La Gomera, which was opened in 1999, only serves inter-insular flights and does not provide viable figures for tourist arrivals. (Binter, 2004) According to an estimation of the harbour authorities of La Gomera, about 65% of the total number of arrivals is excursionists coming from Tenerife to visit the island in one day, 25% is tourists staying on La Gomera and 10% local population.

---

[22] ISTAC 2005

Duration of the stay

The duration of the stay varies according to the nationality of the tourists. Due to the distance from continental Europe, La Gomera is not considered a short trip destination even though this trend is also reaching the Canary Islands and the average period of stay has diminished. Tourists coming from Great Britain often stay only a short period as low budget airlines serve the island of Tenerife. In 2002 the average length of stay of all tourists on Canary Islands was 10.85 days. A difference could be observed between British tourists, who spend less than the average, and Germans and Austrians staying more than 13 days. (CES, 2003, 113) The average length of stay in rural accommodation is shorter. In 2002 the average period in rural accommodation was 7.09 days and in 2003 it was 9.45 days. (ISTAC, 2005)

On La Gomera, the average stay in rural accommodation was with 5.61 days in 2003, which is even below the average of all islands. (Ecotural, 2004, 139) This can maybe be explained by the high percentage of national tourists, of which nearly 70% come from other Canary Islands. Especially people from Tenerife and Grand Canary Island tend to spend their holidays on La Gomera. (Ecotural, 2004, 142)

Nationality

The nationality of tourists in a destination can be an indication regarding the degree of cultural difference between the local population and the tourists. As La Gomera is visited mostly by national tourists and Europeans, one can assume that there is no "cultural clash", but differences still exist. Any assumption in this respect has to be made cautiously as the "tourist culture" not only depends on the nationality, but also on the attitude of people when travelling, along with other factors.

The tourist nationality mix on La Gomera and the rest of the Canary Islands shows differences. In 2003, the Canary Islands counted 9,836,785 international tourist arrivals (not including Spanish tourists). The distribution shows an important concentration on tourists from the United Kingdom (41.28%) and Germany (27.9%). (ISTAC, 2004, 22) According to a different source national tourists, Germans and British counted for 77.6% of the total number of tourists on the Canary Islands. (CES, 2003, 109)

The situation on La Gomera is similar, but with a concentration on the domestic and on the German (instead of the British) market, even though a comparison is not possible due to a lack of data on tourist arrivals in La Gomera.

As no reliable information on tourist arrivals and their nationality is provided on an insular level, the only figures available concern rural tourism and these were elaborated by Ecotural Gomera. In 2003, 61% of the reservations for rural houses on La Gomera were made by domestic tourists (Spain), 14% by Germans, 7% coming from Netherlands, 6% from the United Kingdom and 5% from France. (Ecotural, 2004) On all the Canary Islands in 2003, 23,667 visitors stayed in rural accommodation of which about 38% were Spanish and 62% international tourists. (ISTAC, 2005) A strong concentration on domestic tourism can therefore be recognised.

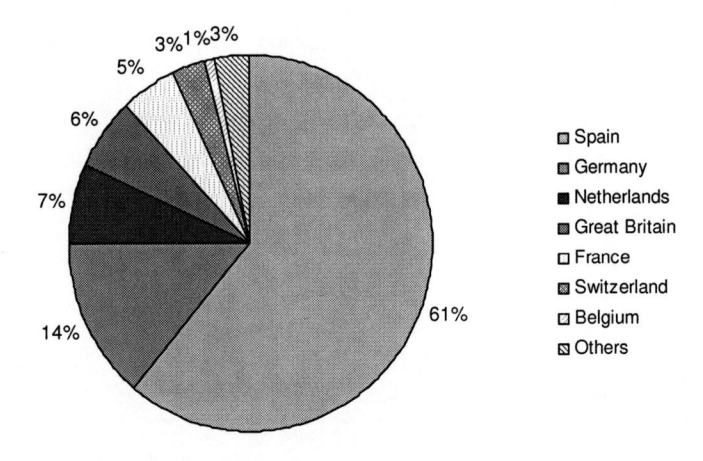

Figure 17: Nationality of rural tourism on La Gomera 2003[23]

6.4.2 Economic indicators

As in all European countries, the concentration on the service sector has modified the economic structure in the Canary Islands. Nowadays the service sector stands for about 78% of the total production on the Canary Islands and the tourism industry is the most important sector of the economy. (CES, 2003, 105) On La Gomera, this process started

---

[23] Ecotural (2004), 138

very late and the change was from an agriculture-dependent directly to a service-based economy, skipping the intermediate industrialisation phase.

Employment in tourism

According to official data, about 74% of all employment on the Canary Islands is in the service industry. (CES, 2003, 105) About 20% of the active population on La Gomera is directly or indirectly employed in tourism. Compared with other Canary Islands, the situation on La Gomera is like on Tenerife and on Gran Canary, the percentage is higher on Fuerteventura and Lanzarote and lower on El Hierro and La Palma. (CES, 2003, 116)
During the last decades, the numbers of active population have increased on all islands due to the incorporation of women in the labour market and due to the high level of immigration. This situation of course has created high pressure on the labour market and has lead to an increase of the unemployment rate. (CES, 2003, 301-305)
The institute of statistics of the Canary Islands published a number of all employment created in rural accommodation of 973 employees in July 2004. (ISTAC, 2005) Considering the number of rural accommodation establishments on the Canary Islands (626 in 2004), an average of 1.5 jobs are created in one rural tourism entity. Rural tourism is not a high potential employment creator but provides the possibility for additional earnings.

The ratio *Employment per Tourist bed* reflects the number jobs created by tourism. This indicator can be restricted to direct employment, but may also be amplified to include indirect employment created by tourism and is an interesting benchmark tool.
Another interesting ratio, with respect to socio-economic impacts, is the number of *Tourism properties owned by local people per tourism properties owned by foreigners*. If the result of this ratio is greater than one, more tourism businesses are owned by foreign investors. Such a situation can result in a leakage of tourism income in the destination.
The indicator of *immigrant workforce per local workforce* analyses the nationality of people employed in the tourism sector. Tourism is often generalised as an employment creator, but the number of local community members employed and in which positions has to be examined in detail. The industry often favours migrant workers who come preferably from the major tourist sending regions, leaving less paid jobs for the local population.

According to a market study of rural tourism conducted by Ecotural Gomera, the following estimation of tourism businesses offering leisure activities on the island can be made. According to the following table, a total of 104 tourism businesses operate on La Gomera. Most fall into the category of motorised activities, 68 agents offer hiking tours, while sporting activities are limited to maritime leisure activities. An interesting fact is that 58% of all businesses operating on La Gomera are not based on the island, hence the generated tourism income does not stay on the island and is withdrawn from the local economy.

Leisure activities	Estimated n° of businesses	Business created and based on La Gomera
Hiking	68	16
Motor-Cycling	4	4
Maritime excursions	5	5
Scubadiving	3	3
Excursions	2	2
Coach lines	4	4
Jeep trips	9	1
Car rental	9	9
TOTAL	104	44

Table 7: Tourism businesses on La Gomera offering leisure activities[24]

Development of the economic sectors

The change of the economic structure on the Canary Islands has severe repercussions on the employment situation. Traditional activities such as agriculture and craftwork have mostly lost their viability and attraction. This development can be illustrated by showing the decrease of employment in those sectors. The following table presents the total number of the working population on all Canary islands and the percentages of people employed in agriculture or service sector. Whereas in 1977, more than 20% of the total population was employed in agriculture, today's rate lies around 4%.

Economic sectors	1977	2003
Total working population	444,430	870,160
Agriculture	20.33%	4.49%
Service Industry	53.66%	78.10%

Table 8: Development of employment according to economic sectors on the Canary Islands[25]

---

[24] Ecotural (2004), 65

Another particularity regarding the economic changes is that the economy of the Canary Islands has changed almost directly from agriculture to the service industry without passing the intermediate stage of industrialisation. Considering the GDP this development becomes even more evident. In 1960, the service sector covered only 44% of the GDP, in 1994 already 79%. The primary sector developed contrarily; in 1960 it made up 32% of the GDP, in 1994 only 4%. (Centro de la cultura popular Canaria, 55f)

On La Gomera the situation is even more significant. In 1969, 80% of the active population of the island worked in the agriculture and fishing industry, 6% in the second sector and 13.99% in the service industry. According to another source, in 1975 the percentage of people working in the primary sector had already declined to 53%. (Reyes Aguilar, 2002, 89) The population census of 2001 (ISTAC, 2005), showed that 70% of the total active population (5,879 people) on La Gomera were employed in the service sector. About 40% of the total working population was employed in tourism related industries, hospitality and restoration.

Employment on La Gomera	Total	Percent
Agriculture and Fishing	358	6.1
Industry	220	3.7
Construction	1,124	19.1
Service	4,152	70.6
Total	5,879	

Table 9: Employment on La Gomera in 2001[26]

6.4.3 Social and cultural indicators

Social and cultural indicators are not as easily defined as economic indicators. Social aspects are mostly linked to other factors, such as economic development, the situation of education, population density and seasonality. Due to this dependency, it is a challenge to isolate social factors and to show development in numeric terms. Cultural indicators are even more subjective and tend to be expressed by the number of cultural manifestations, the extinction of cultural elements and participation in traditional events.

---

[25] after ISTAC (2005)
[26] after ISTAC (2001)

Education

The average level of education on La Gomera is below the European average. This is mainly due to the limited education on offer in the island. In order to study at university level, people are forced to go to La Laguna (Tenerife) or Las Palmas (Grand Canary Island). Nowadays many young people leave the island in order to study or work on the major islands.

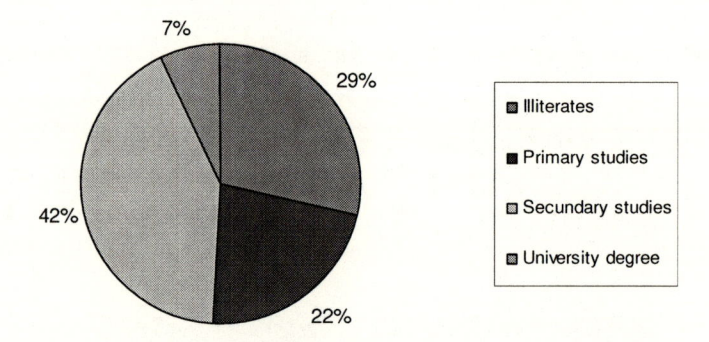

Figure 18: Finalised studies of the population older than 16 of La Gomera (2003)[27]

The figure reflects the situation of education on La Gomera, showing the finished studies of the population older than 16 years. The high degree of illiteracy (29 %) is mainly among the older generation. 22% of the population are recoded as having finished primary education and 42% have a secondary diploma. Only 7% have accomplished university studies.

Tourism density

The main tourism area of La Gomera is the southern part, including the municipalities of San Sebastian, Alajeró and Valle Gran Rey. The table below illustrates the tourism density of the six municipalities of La Gomera.

---

[27] after ISTAC (2004), 9

In total 5,457 beds are provided in the municipalities of the south, which makes up 92% of the total offer in 2002. On La Gomera 12,936 habitants live in the southern part of the island which makes up 68% of the total population. The municipality with the highest *tourist-to-local ratio* is Valle Gran Rey where there are 81.8 tourist beds for every 100 locals. The lowest *tourist-to-local ratio* is calculated for the municipalities of Agulo and Vallehermoso where there are about six tourist beds for every 100 local people.

Municipalities	Population	km²	Total tourist beds	bed/100 hab	beds/km²
Agulo	1160	25.39	72	6.21	2.84
Hermigua	2120	39.67	231	10.90	5.82
Vallehermoso	2775	109.32	170	6.13	1.56
San Sebastian	7437	113.59	1829	24.59	16.10
Alajero	1406	49.42	280	19.91	5.67
Valle Gran Rey	4093	32.36	3348	81.80	103.46
TOTAL	**18990**	**369.75**	**5930**	**31.23**	**16.04**

Table 10: Tourism density referring to the local population on La Gomera 2001[28]

A second indicator regarding tourism density on the island is the *tourist bed/km²*, calculated as a total of the island. In Valle Gran Rey, an average of 103 tourist beds is located on each square kilometre. La Gomera has a tourism density of 16.04 tourist beds per square kilometre.

Certain indicators can not be restricted to the rural tourism sector, but include all forms of tourism on offer. As the tourism density affects everybody and is a phenomenon that does not depend on the type of tourism, the analysis includes the all types of tourism on offer in La Gomera.

Number of foreign residents

In 2003 La Gomera counted a total of 19,580 residents, of which 8.6 % were foreign residents. Of those 1,691 non-Spanish people, 71% came from other countries of the European Union, followed by people from America (20,4%), the rest of Europe and Africa. (ISTAC, 2004, 9) The number of foreign residents has since been increasing. In 1996 a total of 3,973 immigrants lived on La Gomera; 53% came from other Canary Islands, 10%

---

[28] after ISTAC (2005)

from the Spanish mainland and only 36% were foreigners (1,430). A concentration of foreigners living on La Gomera can be observed in Valle Gran Rey. (ICE, 1996, 117)

Number of second homes

The percentage of second homes in a community is an important indicator for social as well as economic impacts. Second homes are only occupied during certain periods throughout the year, so apart from the economic implications this brings, this also means that participation in the social and cultural life of the community is limited to that time.

Tourist motivation

What are tourists looking for? The answer to this question has a high influence on the tourists' behaviour and attitude, "[...] motives are the starting point of the decision making process that leads to particular type of behaviour". (Manson, 2003, 7) Intercultural exchange in tourism destinations is therefore highly influenced by the motivation of tourists.

According to the findings obtained in the market study conducted by Ecotural Gomera, the main motives for tourists to chose La Gomera as a rural holiday destination are its landscape and nature, its quietness and peacefulness, its climate and its non-massified character. These aspects are already followed by cultural motives such as gastronomy, contact with the local population, folklore and celebrations. (Ecotural, 2004, 151)

Rate of hosts and tourists satisfied

In order to obtain valid information on satisfaction levels, ongoing surveys have to be conducted among local residents and visitors. Only tendencies observed in the long term can serve as reliable indicators.
Ecotural Gomera conducted such a survey within the scope of the market study of rural tourism on the island. Of all tourists that filled out the questionnaire, about 95% declared that they would like to spend their holidays again on La Gomera.

Regarding the contact with the local population, 35% declared that it was stimulating and 65% described it as normal. An interesting finding was that international tourists (language difficulties are more likely to occur in this group) indicated the contact to be normal more often (70%). (Ecotural, 2004, 160)

Strength of artistic and folkloric practices

This indicator refers to the development of cultural and traditional activities on the island. Investigations have to be made about the number of people working in traditional and artistic craftwork and the participation level in folklore activities and cultural manifestations such as traditional dance, music and so on.

The development of the associative structure on La Gomera can indicate the level of participation and preoccupancy of the local population regarding cultural issues. According to a listing published by the island authorities in 2004, a total of 37 associations deal with socio-cultural issues.

Type of organisation	Number
Cultural organisations	19
Folklore associations	5
Traditional craftwork	1
Socio-cultural associations	3
Traditional sports	1
Agriculture associations and cooperatives	9
Rural Tourism and Environment	4
Social associations	9
Neighbourhood	9
Youth associations	7
Total	67

Table 11: Social and cultural organisations on La Gomera[29]

The listing can neither be regarded as being exhaustive but should serve as a reflection of the associative structure of La Gomera.

Marketing of the tourist destination

In this respect, the promotion and marketing of the island has to be considered in order to analyse the image created of the destination. How a destination is promoted has a great

---

[29] Cabildo insular (2004)

influence on the expectations of the visitors. It can reinforce stereotypes and influence the behaviour of the tourists during the stay in the destination. Erroneous or exaggerated imaging creates clichés and can, in the long term, put the local population into the situation of playing a role in order to correspond to the promoted image.

6.4.4 Sustainability Index of La Gomera

The following table is a proposal for a sustainability index regarding social and cultural aspects on La Gomera. It summarises the results obtained throughout this chapter.

Indicator	Value
Ratio of vacational tourists/day-trippers	estimated 2.66
Average duration of the stay	5.16 days
Nationality mix	Spain 61% German 14% Netherlands 7% Great Britain 6%
Number of employment in tourism	No figures available
Tourist beds/employment	No figures available
Tourism businesses locals/foreigners	44/60
Tourism employment locals/immigrants	No figures available
Tourism density tourists to local population	31.32/100
Tourist beds/km^2	16.04
Number of foreign residents	1,691
Number of 2nd homes	No figures available
Tourist motivation	Landscape Quietness, Peacefulness Climate
Host and tourist satisfaction	95% wish to return
Number of active craft workers	Official register
Number of social / cultural associations	37

Table 12: List of social and cultural sustainability indicators of La Gomera[30]

---

[30] elaboration by the author

6.4.5 Findings from the indicator analysis

Indicators require further explanation, interpretation or external and internal benchmarks in order to deliver reliable results that can be used for decision making.

There is a series of factors supporting the development of socially and culturally sustainable rural tourism on La Gomera, but there are also other factors hindering this development. La Gomera is not suffering from negative seasonality impacts and is appropriate for all year long activities. The concentration on national tourism in the rural tourism sector reduces cultural differences and negative effects, such as *acculturation*. Another factor enhancing sustainable development is the motivation of rural tourists which creates a favourable basis for cultural exchange and communication. It can be argued that for the major part of tourists coming to La Gomera, cultural elements create an added value to their overall experience. In other words, they are looking for cultural experiences during their holidays and want to get in contact with the local culture and population. The satisfaction level of rural tourists is extremely high.

The short length of stay might be a factor mitigating sustainable development, as tourists don't have enough time to gain in depth experience and adapt to the local culture and lifestyle. The geographic concentration of tourism development causes an unbalanced economic development on the island. Furthermore, it leads to the creation of "tourist ghettos" in the south and villages with a high level of foreigners, hence the cultural and social balance gets lost. With respect to economic issues, it has to be mentioned that the economic change from agriculture towards the service sector can not be stopped, but gradual development that allows people to adapt to the new situation would be more sustainable. The sector of agriculture in its traditional form is not viable anymore, hence a diversification of the economy is necessary. The lack of local initiatives and young businesses constitutes a problem, as most tourism entities operating on La Gomera are based outside the island or owned by foreigners. This situation leads to economic leakages and social problems as the income from tourism is not reinvested in the destination where it is generated. As a consequence, a number of tourism players only have economic interests on La Gomera and maybe do not sufficiently consider negative impacts for the island and its social, cultural and natural environment.

6.5 Tourism Players on La Gomera

Tourism players are referred to as stakeholders, people or entities involved in the tourism development of a destination including public administration, NGOs as well as promoters, travel agencies and tour operators, tourism businesses and non tourism agents such as associations, the local population and tourists themselves.

Public administration is a key player, influencing tourism issues on its distinctive levels. On La Gomera, public administration is based on four levels, the national level, the autonomous area of the Canary Islands, La Gomera and the local level of the communities.

Due to the autonomous status of the Canary Islands, all legislative power for tourism lies within the autonomous governments. Together with the tourism council, the government carries out a series of functions, such as the planning and support of tourism development, the regulation of accommodation and additional tourism offers, the promotion of the destination's image and the conservation and regulation of tourism resources. (Ecotural, 2004, 56-59)

The *Cabildo insular* is the highest authority on the insular level and the most important with regards to rural tourism. The tourism council and the official tourism office, *Patronato de Turismo*, hold specific functions regarding the planning, the support and promotion of tourism. Within the scope of the PTE and the PIO, development plans for La Gomera, territory regulations and development of infrastructure on insular level are defined. Furthermore the island authority decides on laws and controls the legalisation of tourism businesses. The local communities have little legislative power regarding tourism development, but have to approve regulations and development plans.

Ecotural Gomera is an association, founded in 2001 thanks to an initiative of several proprietors of rural houses. Its objectives are the promotion and commercialisation of about 60 associated rural houses via the internet and the reservation centre, the representation of the interests of its members and the association, and the support an balanced development of rural tourism as well as the enhancement of the environmental quality of the houses. Ecotural Gomera is an integrated part of the organisation ACANTUR which promotes rural tourism on all of the Canary Islands. (Ecotural, 2004, 61f)

Ecotural Gomera was founded as a parallel or complementary organisation of the C.I.T. Centre of initiatives and rural tourism of La Gomera which was founded in 1994 by local community members worried about the social and economic development of the north of the island. The C.I.T. participated actively in the first phase of rural tourism development on the island. Today, the tasks of the C.I.T. are the associative evolution and collaboration between proprietors of rural houses and entrepreneurs in other economic sectors and the fulfilment of quality improvement programs and environmental activities. (Ecotural, 2004, 62f)

Aider – Asociación Insular de Desarrollo Rural, the insular association for rural development, plays an important role as an organisation implementing the European development program LEADER II and LEADER +. A main objective is the creation of synergies among the agents of rural development. Furthermore, other topics worked on are the establishment of a new form of relationship between nature, culture and modernity and the creation of a base for a new ecosystem and a new social, cultural and economic balance on La Gomera. (Ecotural, 2004, 68f)

The public administration structure on La Gomera is very complex due to the autonomous status of the Canary Islands. This situation results in a rigid organisation with long communication channels. According to Gomeran experts, (Expert questionnaire, 2005) efforts are made by the public administration to enhance sustainable development but in a limited, uncoordinated and unbalanced manner. One expert is of the opinion that the actions of the public authorities are based mainly on political thinking, leaving sustainable considerations neglected.

As to the non governmental organisations on La Gomera, efforts exist and programs are carried out, but with limited resources. A lack of cooperation and collaboration exists between public and private organisations.

6.6 SWOT Analysis of Rural Tourism on La Gomera

The definition of strengths, weaknesses, opportunities and threats for rural tourism on La Gomera (considered to be a favourable concept for future tourism development) is based on the opinion of local tourism experts. (Ecotural, 2004) The following points present the aspects mentioned by the experts with an emphasis on the issues regarding social and cultural life on the island.

Strengths

The existence of an associative structure in the field of rural tourism with the organisations *Ecotural Gomera* and *Isla rural* is certainly an advantage, but is also considered as an opportunity for improvement. Rural tourism fosters activities in protected areas (National Park of Garajonay) and actions to protect the natural environment. The recuperation of traditional rural architecture is part of the philosophy of rural tourism and prevents the destruction of cultural heritage. It creates business opportunities for residents in rural areas and as a consequence hinders the rural exodus towards the capital city or other islands. For people engaged in agriculture, rural tourism may create an additional income and allows people to remain in their usual settlements and to carry out their traditional activities. In this context, one can argue that rural tourism may revitalise the rural area without negatively affecting traditional activities.

Weaknesses

The sector of rural tourism on La Gomera is still in its infancy and is characterised by a series of weaknesses and a high potential for development. All experts agree that individualism, and economic or capitalist criteria, predominate in most cases of tourism initiatives and that there is a lack of associative thinking. Another important issue emerged with regards to the local administration and government. According to the experts, the non-existence of a legal set of criteria for rural tourism and sustainable development, the lack of institutional support, both in economic but also regulative terms and the absence of realistic data and information about rural tourism are some of the main problems.

Furthermore, a lack of coordination and cooperation exists among the agents involved in the public and private sector. Another weakness linked to the previous points is the fact that development is based on heavy infrastructure financed by public investments and EU subsidies, instead of on local and small scale initiatives. Furthermore, there are severe administrative barriers when it comes to legalising a business and this leads to a high percentage of illegal rural tourism offers.

Another important issue that comes up in the questionnaire is the low level of business management education for local entrepreneurs as well as the lack of enterprises capable to renovate and revitalise old houses to a high standard of quality. In more general terms, the local population has a low understanding of the importance of rural tourism as being a key sector for future development. This leads to a disinterested and passive attitude towards rural tourism in the local population. Additionally, the consciousness of the population with respect to the preservation of the environment is not yet very developed and there is a lack of administrative action with regards to the preservation of the natural environment.

The need for integration of other economic sectors (agriculture, craftwork, culture, etc.) in the tourism, and on the other hand, the inexistence of additional leisure activities are stated clearly. Furthermore, the hybrid character of architectural and ethnographical heritage is an issue mentioned in the questionnaire, referring to the import of foreign cultures in the different offers of tourism (decoration, gastronomy,...).

The oligopoly transport situation of La Gomera, referring to the multinational Fred Olsen serving Los Christianos (Tenerife) and San Sebastián de La Gomera, is also mentioned together with the high number of day-trippers visiting the island on a daily basis. Furthermore the erroneous image of La Gomera which is promoted on the major neighbouring island, selling La Gomera as a sort of "theme park" is pointed out. (Ecotural, Encuesta Delphi) Finally, the image of La Gomera as an island of Christopher Columbus, which is promoted very strongly on the international level, is seen as a garbling of the rich history of the island.

Opportunities

The opportunities for rural tourism development on La Gomera are very promising as there is high potential for development. One has to differentiate internal opportunities, such as resources not yet recognised and external opportunities, such as the evolution of the tourism market.

The concept of rural tourism as it has been developed on La Gomera so far is restricted to accommodation but there is a wide range of opportunities for other activities linked to the rural area. The experts mentioned the rich and retrievable variety of cultural heritage as a support for rural tourism, the enormous range of rural ethnography which has been well preserved and the unique and little known cuisine which are only a few issues that constitute possibilities for the creation of a offer of holistic tourism combined with traditional assets. Rural tourism builds an opportunity to revitalise the rural areas of the island by integrating and cooperating with traditional activities (agriculture, craftwork, etc.). The local input of goods and services used in tourism should be maximised in order to support and integrate the local economy and increase the multiplier effect of the tourism sector., The development of rural tourism offers a wide range of new business opportunities to be based on private, small scale initiatives, especially for the rural population working in traditional sectors.

External factors that create opportunities for rural tourism on La Gomera are primarily the geographic location within a well established and known tourism destination. The differentiation of the major island Tenerife, which is known mostly for conventional tourism, is certainly an opportunity. Tourism development on La Gomera has not yet reached unmanageable levels and the small size of the island constitutes an adequate dimension for rural tourism. There is furthermore a limited risk of an inappropriate increase in the tourism infrastructure in the northern part of the island, which ensures an ideal environment for rural tourism.

The general tendency in tourism of increasing market shares of alternative tourism products such as quality tourism, health tourism and nature based leisure activities, favours the development of La Gomera as a rural tourism destination.

Threats

The experts see one of the main risks as uncontrolled foreign investment. This would mean the loss of the initial philosophy of rural tourism which is based on small scale, local initiatives. Furthermore the carrying out of inappropriate tourism concepts in rural areas is seen as a major risk for La Gomera; some examples mentioned are the "turismo asimilable" (Expert questionnaire, 2005), day-tripping and of course the development of conventional mass tourism in the south of the island. The lack of support from the government and local administration represents a risk when it comes to the creation of an insular development plan. The illegal offers of rural tourism due to bureaucratic barriers may become a problem in future. A threat is also the competition with other islands focusing on rural tourism in a more organised way, like La Palma and El Hierro.

Further threats stated by the experts refer to the local population of La Gomera. The loss of traditions, ethnographical values, local products and craftwork may be a consequence of uncontrolled tourism development. Another is the alteration of the authentic culture due to the imitation of conventional tourism destinations with regards to tourism services offered.

Findings from the SWOT-Analysis

This final part focused on drawing a realistic picture of the situation of rural tourism on La Gomera. There is the threat of loss of heritage and *acculturation* recognised by all experts, as well as the definite need for legal regulations, general planning and organisation. Also other issues have to be pointed out, such as the lack of available data, the inexistent cooperation among the stakeholders, the low level of entrepreneurship among the local population and the inexistence of supplementary touristic offers. The encouraging fact is that many of the threats and weaknesses are also mentioned as an opportunity such as the potential for new business based on cultural heritage and traditional activities and the revitalisation of rural areas, and so on.

The potential for future development is highest when most of the threats can be turned from opportunities and weaknesses into strengths. The process of achieving this situation starts with a detailed knowledge of the current situation and the main problems, to find the definition of commonly accepted goals and appropriate management strategies that are always accompanied by continuous monitoring of development. Prerequisites for successful planning are cooperation and collaboration among all stakeholders, the availability of appropriate data and information, as well as the integration of the local population.

Social and cultural impact analysis for La Gomera

Social Impacts of Rural Tourism on La Gomera

Benefits	Costs
- Increase of the quality of life of the local population, stimulating the development and improvement of infrastructure, installations and services for public use. - Higher mobility on the social ladder. - Creation of recreational infrastructure for public use - Creates education possibilities and equalises the levels of formation among the population - Increase of income - Improved technology - Tourism revenues can be invested in other sectors - Lowers the level of emigration as it creates future perspectives	- Creation of tourism *ghettos* - Social tension due to the introduction of foreign workforce - Increased prices for land and housing - Unbalanced distribution of income from tourism - Tourism does not permit the existence of other economic sectors in an area - Acculturation effects, especially among the young people

Figure 19: Social Impacts of Rural Tourism on La Gomera[31]

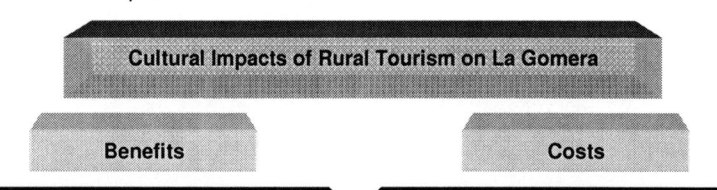

Cultural Impacts of Rural Tourism on La Gomera

Benefits	Costs
- Positive cultural changes in terms of tolerance, open mindedness, etc. - Communication and intercultural exchange between tourists and local population - Hybrid cultures - Tourism investment can be used for cultural activities such as festivals, courses etc. - Promotion of the local culture in other countries - More consciousness about the value of local culture	- Commercialisation of cultural elements - Manipulation and exploitation of the historic and ethnographic heritage - Changes in traditional architecture - Degradation of the traditions, increase of marginal groups and criminal behaviour (prostitution, drug addiction, robbery) - Loss of cultural identity/authenticity and cultural uprooting - Decrease of the value of traditional craftwork (souvenirs)

Figure 20: Cultural Impacts of Rural Tourism on La Gomera[32]

---

[31] Expert Questionnaire (2005)
[32] Expert Questionnaire (2005)

7 SUGGESTIONS FOR ACTION

Taking into account the previous analysis of the situation, in the following chapter recommendations for improvement shall be presented. The overall goal of the suggested actions is the creation of a favourable environment for sustainable tourism without mitigating social and cultural development on La Gomera.

The recommended program for improvement is based on three main pillars:

- Education and information
- Local participation
- Research and monitoring

In order to reach a satisfactory level of development, the main strategies have to be supported by all stakeholders and accompanied by a series of complementary actions. Education in this respect refers to educational programs for the local population in order to allow them to compete on the international market. On the other hand, information for tourists is an important issue as well as information regarding the local population. The objective is to increase awareness about the impacts of tourism. Local participation is *the* key factor, as any development has to be supported by, and initiated by, the local population. The lack of information and data concerning tourism is a major weakness on La Gomera, hence a holistic tourism information system should be implemented in order to provide viable data for decision making and long term planning. Cooperation and coordination are prerequisites in order to successfully realise any program for improvement. For enhanced communication among all stakeholders, a round table for tourism will be proposed as a platform for sustainable tourism development.

"An important policy is to develop tourism on a gradual basis which allows residents time to adapt to it, as well as time to monitor the social (and environmental) impacts [...]". (WTO, 2001, 131) Sustainable development on La Gomera has been going on for about one decade and still basic requirements are failing, such as the recycling process and waste disposal, sustainable use of water resources and the implementation of sewage plants. Furthermore, the educational system has to be adapted in order to provide education and formation for all age groups. It takes time to change peoples' attitudes and behaviour. On La Gomera, the development of tourism should not be accelerated in order to give the local community time to adapt and take part in the development of their island as a tourism destination. A gradual and controlled growth that favours small scale business based on local initiatives has to be guaranteed.

As a first step, it is important to distribute responsibilities of the single tourism players, the government, the public administration and the private sector. Cooperation and collaboration among all stakeholders are essential for a successful development. The public administration usually has the tasks of policy making, planning and research, provision of infrastructure, establishing of land use plans, environmental protection regulations, tourism education, offering incentives to attract private sector investments, maintaining public safety, as well as some marketing functions. (WTO, 2001, 98) Private sector enterprises provide tourism services such as accommodation, transport, leisure activities, and information, tour and travel operations. The NGOs can perform research activities and often have a valuable role in assessing tourism enterprises and administration and consulting function.

7.1 The importance of the individual players in tourism

Sustainable tourism development is favourable for the future of La Gomera since, it both supports traditional activities and economic sectors other than tourism, and also improves the living standard of the local population, without damaging the environment.

The general goal has to be split up; specific problems to be solved have to be identified and sub-goals defined. As this work is focused on social and cultural aspects, the main objectives for La Gomera in this respect are:
- Improvement of the employment situation by fostering local entrepreneurship
- Development of a small scale tourism infrastructure with high local employment
- Increase of living standard for the local population and introduction of community facilities
- Networking and cooperation among the economic sectors and stakeholders
- Enhancement of cultural values and community interests
- Improvement of cultural offers for the local population and visitors
- Enhancement of the experience for hosts and visitors

Each tourism player has to know and accept their responsibilities and has to constantly work towards more sustainable development of tourism. Competences and fields of work are attributed according to the responsibility of the single players.

Public authorities

The public authorities have an especially important key function, as overall planning has to be based on a legal framework defined on this level. The insular government has to make sure that sustainability is part of the general development plan for the island and is imposed by legal policies.
"Planning is a forward-looking, future oriented activity. In the past, planning was often a largely reactive process in response to perceived problems." (Manson, 2003, 79) On La Gomera, legal actions are mostly taken as measures of crisis management. The primary objective has to be to change this approach in order to act, instead of reacting.
Public administration has the duty to create or support networks and synergies between different economic sectors. In other words, the multiplier effect should serve as a catalyst for the expansion of other local economic activities.

Financial incentives

Investment aids and support for local entrepreneurs have to be provided in order to encourage local ownership and enhance the establishment of small-scale tourism enterprises based on local initiatives. Motivation and education are especially necessary on La Gomera, where the spirit of entrepreneurship is scarce. (Expert questionnaire, 2005) On European level, subsidies are proposed for rural development, such as the LEADER projects of the European Union which have significantly influenced the development of rural tourism in mainland Spain and Portugal. (Butler, 2001, in Weaver, 2001, 441) Subsidies were used on La Gomera for the construction and adoption of single rural houses, but not for the development of a rural tourism infrastructure in a general sense. Such a development is necessary in order to motivate and support sustainable development in rural areas on La Gomera and create a holistic offer of rural tourism. In this respect it is equally important to set limits on international and non-local investment in the tourism sector on La Gomera in order to reduce economic leakages. Tourism on the island has to be developed gradually in order to give local people the chance to adapt and invest in their own businesses.

Education and information programs

"Educate residents about tourism (public awareness programmes) and tourists about local customs (tourist behaviour code). " (WTO, 2001, 132) Education programs should be established on three levels. First, education has to be provided for local people working in tourism to enable them to compete on the international market. Equally important is that information on the concept of sustainability in tourism and its practical implications is provided for all inhabitants. Second, tourism awareness programs have to inform the local population about characteristics of tourism, trends, benefits, problems and raise awareness concerning ecological problems and other issues. Different media can be used in order to spread the information among the local population. On La Gomera, radio broadcasts, local newspaper articles and community meetings would be especially effective. Cautiousness and feelings of responsibility have to be increased in order to enhance direct participation and concern for ecological and cultural issues on the island. The third level of information addresses the tourists and communicates information regarding social and ecological problems and cultural issues, such as about events and activities. It's important to make tourists aware of the difficulties faced in the holiday destination and explain how they can positively participate in resolving the same.

The cultural education of the local population of the tourism destination is another important aspect in this respect. Administrative efforts to promote and enhance culture on La Gomera offer wide areas of improvement; that is the result of the expert questionnaire conducted within the scope of this work. Furthermore, there is a lack of cooperation and collaboration among the administrative agents and programs offered are disorganised and unbalanced. (Expert questionnaire, 2005) Local dance, music, arts and craftwork in traditional areas have to be preserved and transmitted through training programmes and workshops in which the local population can practise traditional craftwork and cultural expression. Recuperation programs and familiarisation with cultural elements in the form of workshops have to be organised and supported by the public administration. Only a culture lived by the local population is authentic and can be transmitted to the next generations and visitors.

Zoning

Zoning can be used on an insular level, hand in hand with the development of certain indicators for the specific zones. This tool can serve for growth management by applying capacity limits for specific zones. The already existing development plan for La Gomera (PTE) has to be extended, modified and must integrate capacity limits. The overall objective is to capture the benefits of growth, while at the same time mitigate its negative consequences. Such growth management strategies heavily rely on data in the form of indicators to chart progress towards more desirable and sustainable future conditions. (Waldron, Williams, 2002, in Harris, Griffin, Williams, 2002, 186) In the southern part of the island more than elsewhere, certain areas are already very densely populated and show high construction density. The administration has to impede excessive tourism infrastructure development in order to protect the island's ambience and natural landscape. Furthermore, regulations concerning the height of buildings and the architectural style have to be defined in order to preserve the original image of the island.

Non governmental organisations and associations

Non governmental organisations have two main fields of action. These are firstly support of individual businesses, and secondly consultancy for the public authorities.

NGOs should support efforts of individuals, encourage local ownership, stand up for the interest of their members and promote specific issues regarding social and cultural impacts. Furthermore, NGOs should provide appropriate training, education and information in order to sensitise the public and increase awareness on specific issues. Another important task of associations is to strengthen the links between the tourism industry and other economic sectors in order to augment synergies and reduce economic leakages by promoting the use of local products and services. NGOs should provide assistance and consultancy for local people in order to facilitate the opening of a tourism business. Associations for craftwork, folklore and local products should create stamps or labels for the traditional products of La Gomera and promote traditional craftwork. Visitor centres could enhance the promotion of craftworks. The creation of agricultural associations would help in order to promote and sell local products more efficiently.

NGOs should act as a consultancy for the public administration, conduct research and provide analysis on specific issues. Furthermore, they should be integrated in the decision making and planning processes. Specific projects should be outsourced and conducted by NGOs. Certainly, a main issue is the linkage of authorities and population. A further responsibility of NGOs should be the assistance and implementation of certain policies, therefore cooperation has to exist between authorities and the organisations in order to multiply instead of dispersing efforts.

Tourism businesses

Agriculture is becoming economically unviable in many parts of the world and this development especially affects small scale businesses. But still, a "[...] widespread growth in the market for farm produce and particularly organic and natural agricultural produce" can be observed. (Butler, 2001, in Weaver, 2001, 436) As the local economy of La Gomera is still partly based on agriculture, a main objective should be the support of local production by using and promoting local products in tourism businesses. "Arts and crafts tourism is an interesting development in many rural parts of Europe." (Smith, 2003, 79) It can help to revive traditional production methods and therefore has both economic and socio-cultural benefits for the local communities, especially in regions were the agricultural sector has been declining. Creative tourism is gaining importance as people often don't have time for creative expression in their everyday lives. Artistic and handcraft workshops for visitors constitute attractions and at the same time allow local people to transmit their culture and traditional production and at the same time earn their living. Tourism should create potential for other economic sectors instead of hindering their existence. Cooperation with tourism businesses such as hotels, travel agents, tour guides have to be enhanced in order to create networks and synergies. This would lead to an increase in sales and also a stimulation of the agricultural sector and traditional production of La Gomera.

Tourism entities have to focus on the local culture. The offer of tourism has to reflect La Gomera and its cultural particularities instead of imitating imported cultures or a standardised tourism culture. The existence of foreign tourism offers, importing other cultures and cuisines, has to be limited and must not cover the local identity of La Gomera.

The consciousness of people employed in tourism has to be developed regarding their responsibility for the island and the local culture.

7.2 New forms of cooperation

As mentioned earlier, collaboration among the different stakeholders involved in tourism on La Gomera is essential in order to effectively work towards more sustainability and reduce the negative impacts of tourism. In the following, two models of cooperation are presented that treat the most important issues, such as enhanced communication among the different players, integration of the local population and tourism research.

Round Table of Tourism

On La Gomera, communication and cooperation between the different players is a weak point. In order to enhance the finding of a consensus and participative decision making, the creation of a round table of tourism is recommended for La Gomera. This would bring all stakeholders from the public administration, NGOs and tourism businesses together to discuss current issues and enhance cooperation on the insular level. An overall goal is to improve the coordination and networking among all stakeholders and economic sectors on the island which are affected by globalisation and the changing economic situation. "Global integration is creating opportunities for some, nightmares for many. In this juxtaposition of winners and losers, a new strategy for rural development is required, a strategy that re-evaluates the contribution of traditional production strategies." (Barkin, 2005, 6) In other words, tourism on La Gomera has to go hand in hand with other sectors, such as agriculture and traditional productions. Specific actions and programs have to be discussed at the round table for tourism, involving all stakeholders.

The need for organisation and collaboration among the different stakeholders emerged as a key issue from the expert questionnaire. The organisations have to accept their responsibilities in the social and cultural development of the island. All local stakeholders are asked to live and communicate the local culture, as well as create space for intercultural exchange. Another issue mentioned in the expert questionnaire is the enhanced communitarianism, essential for the persistence of authentic cultural activities and celebrations. By inviting tourists to cultural festivities, they get the chance to experience an authentic event, and not a spectacle. (Expert questionnaire, 2005)

Local participation is an important issue in this context. Thanks to enhanced communication and awareness campaigns, the population has to be both addressed and motivated to take part in development and decision making. People have to be encouraged to decide upon the future of the island and take initiatives and positions. "The population is not informed enough to decide and analyse the situation of the island" (Expert questionnaire, 2005) hence transparency and the integration of the population in the entire process are necessary. This could be achieved by nominating representatives that take part in the round table discussions by holding town hall meetings and open discussion forums where the public is invited to communicate their opinions. Also, the media has a key function as its cooperation will decide upon the success or failure of communication with the public.

The figure below illustrates an adapted concept for enhanced social and cultural sustainability on La Gomera. The coordination of the program is centralised and should be realised by an interdisciplinary expert group working closely together with the public authorities. The round table of tourism has to be an integral part of the project from the beginning on, and must serve as a point of consultation for the coordination group. It should participate actively in decision making. This scheme is the quintessence of the last chapters, summarising and illustrating a possible managerial concept to guarantee a more sustainable development of tourism.

Suggestions for Action

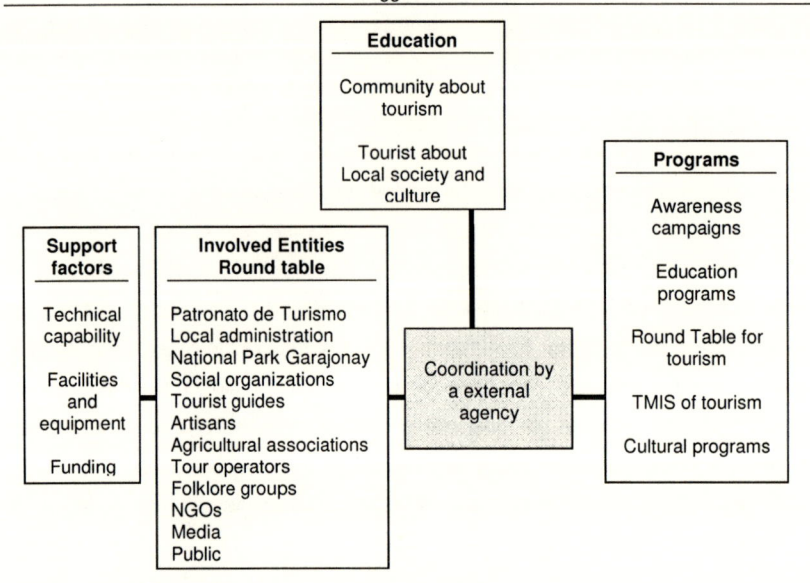

Support factors	Involved Entities Round table		Education	
Technical capability	Patronato de Turismo		Community about tourism	
	Local administration		Tourist about Local society and culture	
	National Park Garajonay	Coordination by a external agency		Programs
Facilities and equipment	Social organizations			Awareness campaigns
	Tourist guides			Education programs
	Artisans			Round Table for tourism
Funding	Agricultural associations			TMIS of tourism
	Tour operators			Cultural programs
	Folklore groups			
	NGOs			
	Media			
	Public			

Figure 21: Organisation structure of social and cultural programs[33]

Tourism information system

A concept for monitoring and control is missing on La Gomera. No research on tourism and on the consequences of tourism development has been conducted so far. A holistic system for long term assessment is necessary to ensure a viable analysis of the situation and future tendencies.

Tourism research on the public level is important in order to provide a basis for decision making, long term planning, benchmarking, monitoring and impact control. In this respect the implementation of a tourism management information service (TMIS) is recommended. Cooperation among all the stakeholders is necessary in order to feed a database with the most accurate data. Thanks to continuous data collection, trends and development can be analysed in order to assess and monitor impacts. The TMIS is usually made up of data about tourist arrivals, satisfaction levels, number of visitors to tourism attractions, accommodation types and occupancy rates, economic data as well as environmental and social indicators. (WTO, 2001, 143f) The implementation, coordination and maintenance of a TMIS have to lie within the responsibility of the public authorities or an expert agency,

---

[33] after Inskeep (1991), in WTO (2001), 134 and Expert questionnaire (2005)

and be based within a legal framework. The data collection has to be made in cooperation with different tourism agents on the island, such as tourism businesses, the regional and local governments, tourism operators, communities, interest groups and NGOs. Of course, the accuracy and checking of the entered data is important in order to ensure the viability of the results. Thanks to this tourism database, all information can be treated centrally, ensuring transparency and regular communication of results.

An easily manageable and understandable set of indicators has to be developed in order to monitor the impacts of tourism on the island's ecosystem, the economic situation and of course, social structure and cultural development. During a "visioning phase" the local population and experts are involved in the program and equally participate in the planning. By conducting surveys, organising town hall meetings, seminars, workshops and focus groups, the overall goals should be set and accepted by all interest groups.

With respect to the target groups addressed by the results of the indicator program, three different groups are determined. Firstly, the information obtained should be used for awareness campaigns addressing the local population in order to make them more conscious about the ongoing and future development of the island. This can often be a long process, but with accurate information campaigns and community discussions, awareness, sensitivity and concern will arise. Finally, all stakeholders in tourism should get access to the data obtained in order to provide a detailed vision of the sector. Of course, public administration and regional government should make use of the information obtained in order to take any necessary measures for improvement and future planning.

8   FINAL CONCLUSIONS

The presented work provides a theoretic approach and an attempt to implement practically certain concepts on La Gomera. It tends to present and combine two complementary approaches treating the complex issues of the social and cultural impacts of tourism, literature based research and practical investigation.

A major finding of the work is the generally positive correlation that exists between society and cultural development and sustainable tourism. Throughout the work, the importance of management and planning approaches is pointed out in order to mitigate any negative impacts that might occur.
In order to conclude the case study of La Gomera, certain aspects have to be pointed out. The suggestions made in the last chapters must not be understood as a model of resistance for La Gomeran culture, but rather as a series of suggestions to support the protection of cultural heritage, foster the social and cultural life of the local population and at the same time enhance intercultural exchange between tourists and hosts. The cultural identity of La Gomera has always been characterised by external influences as well as its geographic isolation, and has always been subject to change. On La Gomera, culture is irrevocably linked to rural traditions and the rural way of life. Important issues of the Gomeran identity are the Silbo, the forest, the sea, the rural landscape, the music and folklore, hence only a holistic concept of tourism development for the island, integrating the rural culture and the traditional way of life in a modern concept of development, is appropriate to keep authentic culture alive.

With respect to the social impacts, the most important finding was the need to support and motivate the local population of La Gomera to take initiatives and participate in the development of their living environment. On the other hand, a gradual development of tourism based on small scale locally owned business, such as rural tourism, would be highly recommendable. In order to foster such development, full support has to be guaranteed from part of the public authorities. Primary necessities are the creation of a favourable legal framework, limiting non-local investment and encouraging local entrepreneurship.

Cultural development has to go its natural course, following its own pace. In other words it must not be stopped (nostalgic factors) nor accelerated (*acculturation*) by, or for, tourism.

Conclusions

A series of cultural management strategies is presented within the scope of this work, based on awareness programs and educational measures addressed to hosts and tourists. The population has to appreciate, know and live their culture. It will then automatically be communicated to visitors. It is therefore crucial to facilitate space and occasions for intercultural exchange between tourists and hosts. Only a lived culture can be transmitted authentically.

Intercultural exchange and getting to know other cultures has always been attractive for a certain type of tourists. This fact has, at the same time, created problems and negative effects in the destinations. The interaction between tourists and hosts can not be planned nor directly influenced. Nevertheless, the creation of a favourable environment for intercultural exchange within the scope of tourism has to be focused on. This can be achieved by appropriate information measures, respectful behaviour and social and economic equity.

The main results about the current situation of rural tourism on La Gomera were obtained by conducting an expert survey in form of a *Delphi questionnaire*. Following the *Delphi method*, ten experts filled out a questionnaire with 15 open questions regarding the social and cultural aspects of rural tourism on La Gomera. The experts were chosen according to their position and involvement in social and cultural issues. Included are the public administration on insular as well as local level, associations and businesses involved in tourism, craft workers and local population. The questionnaire was prepared as a qualitative expert questionnaire with open questions, the evaluation was shown in a summarising form. The overall goal of the questionnaire was the aggregation of ideas and collection of opinions prevailing on the island, hence no claim to representation can be made. The summarised opinions of the experts served to support certain arguments within this work and to elaborate a SWOT analysis of rural tourism with regards to social and cultural issues. It can be said that opportunities exceed the risks that can be turned into strengths. Nevertheless, as it has been pointed out there are several weaknesses disfavouring a sustainable development of rural tourism on La Gomera, such as the lack of a legal framework, the missing integration of other economic sectors and creation of an offer of holistic rural tourism. In the opinion of most experts, a major threat is the accelerated and inappropriate tourism development taking place on the island and the uncontrolled foreign investment in the tourism infrastructure. Due to the fast development of tourism, the local economy which has always been based on agriculture and craftwork, is not able to keep up. The local population has no time to adapt and does therefore not participate in the development of its island.

The suggestions for improvement presented can be summarised in three key issues, (i) information and education, (ii) local participation and (iii) research and investigation. The results obtained from the *Delphi questionnaire* revealed the urgent need for measures to enhance education and information for the local population and visitors, legal regulations, the integration of the local population in the decision making and future planning process and the appropriate information and research necessary to provide viable data, to ensure a favourable development of tourism.

In chapter seven, a series of actions for improvement are suggested. All different stakeholders have to accept their role and actions to be taken are attributed to specific entities. The most important measures to be implemented on La Gomera are:

- Community and tourist education and information
- Space for intercultural exchange and host-guest interaction
- Preservation of local architectural style and limits of construction
- Protection of cultural expression and manifestations as well as local arts
- Strengthening of the linkages between tourism and traditional sectors
- Creation of synergies by promoting the purchase of local goods and services
- Encourage local ownership, limits on non-local investment
- Training and education for the local population
- Gradual development of tourism

Two measures to foster the cooperation among the different stakeholders are proposed in the work in order to cover an urgent need for enhanced collaboration and communication among the different players in tourism. The round table for tourism should serve as a communication platform between public authorities, tourism businesses and other economic sectors, associations and the local population. It should then also serve as a consultancy for the public authorities and have a vote in the decision making process. A holistic, web based and integrative controlling and monitoring system presented in this work shall provide data and information necessary to take decisions about the future development. The system presented is based on the collaboration of all stakeholders and integrates several sources.

Conclusions

This work shall constitute a point of departure for more sustainable thinking in social and cultural terms, demonstrate the importance of certain impacts and the necessity for further research and investigation in this field. Maybe in certain occasions, economic objectives should be lined up behind social and cultural issues in order to prevent the loss of even higher values and to ensure a more people-friendly development.

TABLE OF ABBREVIATIONS

CES	Consejo económico y social de Canarias
CIT	Centro de Iniciativas Turísticas
FRAP	Frequency-relevance analysis of problems
GDP	Gross Domestic Product
IQM	Integrated Quality Management
ISO	International Organisation for Standardisation
ISTAC	Instituto canario de estadísticas
NGO	Non governmental organisation
PIO	Plan Integral de Ordención
PRA	Participative Rural Appraisal
PTE	Plan Territorial Especial
SWOT	Strengths, Weaknesses, Opportunities, Threats
TCC	Tourism Carrying Capacity
TDQ	Total Destination Quality
TIES	The international ecotourism society
TMIS	Tourism management information service
TQM	Total Quality Management
TSQ	Total Service Quality
WTO	World Tourism Organisation

BIBLIOGRAPHY

Books

Binder B.B. (2002); Wechselbeziehungen zwischen Tourismus und der Red-Indianisierung in Cusco, Peten; Bonn: Rhienischen Friedrich-Wilhelms Universität

Boyne S. (2003); New Directions in Rural Tourism Impact Research; in: Hall D.; New directions in rural tourism; Aldershot: Ashgate, 19-35

Dale H. (2003); Total Quality Management; Upper Saddle Ricer: Pentice Hall

Eagles P.F.J., McCool S.F., Haynes C.D. (2002); Sustainable tourism in protected areas: guidelines for planning and management; 1st edition, Gland: IUCN, The World Conservation Union

European Commission (1999); Towards Quality in rural tourism, Integrated Quality Management; <http://europa.eu.int/comm/enterprise/services/tourism-publications/documents/iqm_rural_en.pdf>; access: 08.01.05; 14.50

Fennell D. (1999); Ecotourism: An introduction; London: Routledge

Glasson J., Godrey K., Goodey B. (1995); Towards Visitor Impact Management; 1st edition, Aldershot: Avebury

Häder M. (2002); Delphi-Befragungen; 1st edition; Wiesbaden: Link Westdt.Verl.

Hernández Hernández P. (2000); Conocer Canarias; La Laguna: Tafor Publicaciones

Howforth M., Munt I. (1998); Tourism and Sustainability; 2nd edition, London: Routledge

Ladrón de Guevara Á. (2004); La Gomera 2004; 2nd edition, Los Christianos: Gráficas Los Christianos

Langer M. (1997); Service Quality in Tourism: Measurement Methods and Empirical Analysis; Frankfurt/Main: Lang

Manson P. (2003); Tourism Impacts, Planning and Management; 1st edition, Oxford: Butterworth-Heinemann

Nau P. (1997); Gomera; 3rd edition, Köln: DuMont

Page S.J., Dowling R.K. (2002); Ecotourism; Harlow: Prentice Hall
Perera M.J.L. (2001); Recuperación de Costumbres y Tradiciones de la Isla de La Gomera; Santa Cruz de Tenerife: Imprecan

Reyes Aguilar A. (2002); Estructura agraria, grupos de parentesco y política local en Hermigua (Gomera): Un estudio antropológico local (1900-1980); 1st edition, Arafo: Litografía Romero

Robinson M., Boniface P. (1999); Tourism and Cultural Conflicts; 2nd edition; Oxon: CABI Pub.

Schewe C. D., Hiam A. (1998); The portable MBA in Marketing; 2nd edition, New York: John Wiley & Sons

Smith M.K. (2003); Issues in Cultural Tourism Studies; 1st edition, London: Routledge

Swarbrooke J. (2004); Sustainable tourism management; 1st edition, Wallingford: CABI Pub.

World Tourism Organization (1993); Sustainable Development, Guide for local planners; 1st edition; Madrid: WTO

World Tourism Organization (1996); What tourism managers need to know; Madrid: WTO

World Tourism Organization (2001); Guide for local authorities on developing sustainable tourism; 2nd edition, Madrid: WTO

Articles

Backman S., Petrick J., Wright B.A. (2001); Management Tools and Techniques: an Integrated Approach to Planning; in: Weaver D.B. (ed.); The encyclopaedia of ecotourism; 1st edition, Wallingford: CABI Publ, 451-462

Barkin D. (2005); Ecotourism: A Tool for Sustainable Development in an Era of International Integration; Yale F&ES Bulletin, <http://www.yale.edu/environment/publications/bulletin/099pdfs/99barkin>; access: 09.03.2005 at 13.00

Bodley J.H. (1997); Microsoft Encarta Online Encyclopaedia 2004, Culture; <http://encarta.msn.com/encyclopedia_761561730/Culture.html>; access: 29.12.2004 at 17.53

Brent J.R., Crouch G.I. (1997); Quality, price and the tourism experience: roles and contributions to destination competitiveness; in: Keller P. (ed.); Quality Management in tourism; St. Gall: AIEST, 117-137

Butler R.W. (2001); Rural Development; in: Weaver D.B. (ed.); The encyclopaedia of ecotourism; 1st edition, Wallingford: CABI Publ, 433-446

Coccossis H. (2004); Sustainable Tourism and Carrying Capacity: A new context; in: Coccossis H. (ed.); The challenge of tourism carrying capacity; Aldershot: Ashgate, 3-13

Coccossis H., Mexa A. (2004); Tourism Carrying Capacity: Methodological Considerations; in: Coccossis H. (ed.); The challenge of tourism carrying capacity; Aldershot: Ashgate, 55-89

Diamantis D., Westlake J. (2001); Ecolabelling in the Context of Sustainable Tourism and Ecotourism; in: Font X., Buckley R.C. (ed.); Tourism ecolabelling: certification and promotion of sustainable management; Wallingford: CABI Publ, 27-37

Dowling R.K., Fennell D.A. (2003); The context of ecotourism policy and planning; in: Fennell D.A. (ed.); Ecotourism policy and planning; Wallingford: CABI Pub, 1-15

Epler Wood M. (2002); Developing a Framework to Evaluate Ecotourism as a Conservation and Sustainable Development Tool; <http://www.ecotourism.org/pdf/stanford_framework.pdf>; access: 9.3.2005 at 11.30

Fennell D.A., Dowling R.K. (2003); Ecotourism Policy and Planning: Stakeholders, Management and Governance; in: Fennell D.A. (ed.); Ecotourism policy and planning; Wallingford: CABI Pub, 311-343

Freyer W. (1997); Qualitätsbestimmung für Destinationen: zur Prädikatisierung von "Qualitäts-Erholungsorten" in Deutschland; in: Keller P. (ed.); Quality Management in tourism; St. Gall: AIEST, 251-251

Gortázar L., Marín C. (1999); Herramientas para la gestión del turismo sostenible; in: Revista Canaria de Turismo; 5-1999; Santa Cruz/Tenerife: Gobierno de Canarias, 79-96

Halpenny E.A. (2001); Islands and Coasts; in: Weaver D.B. (ed.); The encyclopaedia of ecotourism; 1st edition, Wallingford: CABI Publ, 235-250

Hardin G. (1977); Ethical Implications of Carrying Capacity; <http://dieoff.org/page96.htm>; access 08.03.2005; 18.00

Hawkins D.E., Lamoureux K. (2001); Global Growth and Magnitude of Ecotourism; in: Weaver D.B. (ed.); The encyclopaedia of ecotourism; 1st edition, Wallingford: CABI Publ, 63-72

Hope C. (1997); What does Quality Managemtn mean for Tourism Companies and Organisations; in: Keller P. (ed.); Quality Management in tourism; St. Gall: AIEST, 59-85

Insula (2005); Islands, putting theory into practice; <http://www.insula.org/tourism/islands2.htm>; access: 09.03.2005 at 13.00

Kaae B.C. (2001); The Perceptions of Tourists and Residents of Sustainable Tourism Principles and Environmental Initiatives; in: Mc Cool (ed.); Tourism, Recreation and Sustainability: Linking Culture and the Environment; New York: CABI Publishing, 289-311

Keller P. (1997); Quality management in tourism: Areas of Inquiry; in: Keller P. (ed.); Quality Management in Tourism; St. Gall: AIEST, 7-13

Lieb M.G. (1997); Strategien des Qualitätsmanagements; in: Pompl W., Dreyer A. (ed.); Qualitätsmanagement im Tourismus; München: Oldenburg, 30-55

Macleod D. (2003); Ecotourism for Rural Development in the Canary Islands and the Caribbean; in: Hall D.; New directions in rural tourism; Aldershot: Ashgate, 194-203

Mexa A., Coccossis H. (2004); Tourism Carrying Capacity: A Theoretical Overview; in: Coccossis H. (ed.); The challenge of tourism carrying capacity; Aldershot: Ashgate, 37-51

Planeta (2005); Definitions Ecotourism; <
http://www.planeta.com/ecotravel/tour/definitions.html>; access: 20.03.2005 at 20.50

Pompl W. (1997); Qualität touristischer Dienstleistungen; in: Pompl W., Dreyer A. (ed.); Qualitätsmanagement im Tourismus; München: Oldenburg, 1-29

Scharitzer D. (1997); Methoden der Qualitätsmessung; in: Pompl W., Dreyer A. (ed.); Qualitätsmanagement im Tourismus; München: Oldenburg, 56-82

Sharpley R. (2001); The Consumer Behaviour Context of Ecolabelling; in: Font X., Buckley R.C. (ed.); Tourism ecolabelling: certification and promotion of sustainable management; Wallingford: CABI Publ, 41-55

Sharpley R. (2003); Rural Tourism and Sustainability – A Critique; in: Hall D.; New directions in rural tourism; Aldershot: Ashgate, 38-51

Sirakaya E., Jamal T.B., Choi H.S. (2001); Developing Indicators for Destination Sustainability; in: Weaver D.B. (ed.); The encyclopaedia of ecotourism; 1st edition, Wallingford: CABI Publ, 411-432

Synergy (2000); Tourism Certification; <http://www.wwf.org.uk/filelibrary/pdf/tcr.pdf>; access: 20.03.2005 at 20.50

TIES, The International Ecotourism Society (2003); A simple user's guide to certification for sustainable tourism and ecotourism; Washington DC:
<http://www.ecotourism.org/index2.php?onlineLib/search.php>; access: 12.06.2004 at 12.45

Waldron D., Williams P.W. (2002); Steps towards sustainability monitoring: the case of the Resort Municipality of Whistler; in: Harris R., Griffin T., Williams P.; Sustainable Tourism, a global perspective; 1st edition, Oxford: Butterworth/Heinemann, 180-193

Wearing S. (2001); Exploring Socio-cultural Impacts on Local Communities; in: Weaver D.B. (ed.); The encyclopaedia of ecotourism; 1st edition, Wallingford: CABI Publ, 395-410

Weiermair K. (1997); On the Concept and Definition of Quality in Tourism; in: Keller P. (ed.); Quality Management in tourism; St. Gall: AIEST, 33-58

Wight P.A. (2001); Ecotourists: Not a Homogeneous Market Segment; in: Weaver D.B. (ed.); The encyclopaedia of ecotourism; 1st edition, Wallingford: CABI Publ, 37-62

Youell R. (2003); Integrated Quality Management in Rural Tourism; in: Hall D.; New directions in rural tourism; Aldershot: Ashgate, 169-181

Studies

Centro de la cultura popular Canaria (1995); Canarias: La Economia; Santa Cruz: Cabildo de Tenerife

CES, Consejo Económico y Social de Canarias (2003); Informe Anual, La Economía, la sociedad y el empleo en Canarias durante el año 2002; 1st edition, Las Palmas: Litografía Prag

Ecotural Gomera (2004); Estudio-Guía para la adecuada implantación del turismo rural en el entorno del parque nacional Garajonay; Hermigua

ICE (1996); Estadistiacas Demograficas, Encuesta de Población Canaria 1996; Las Palmas: Gobierno de Canarias

ISTAC (2001); Censos de población y viviendas de Canarias, 1.11.2001; <http://www.gobiernodecanarias.org/istac/estadisticas.html>; access: 13.03.2005 at 17.30

ISTAC (2004); Canarias en cifras 2003; 1st edition, Las Palmas: ISTAC
ISTAC (2005); Estadísticas por tema;
<http://www.gobiernodecanarias.org/istac/estadisticas.html>; access: 23.01.2005 at 16.00

Izquierdo Trujillo J., Salas Gil J. (1999); Guía básica para la gestión sostenible del turismo en espacios naturales protegidos; Santa Cruz/Tenerife

Kirstges T. (2003); Sanfter Tourismus: Chance und Probleme der Realisierung eines ökologieorientierten und sozialverträglichen Tourismus durch deutsche Reiseveranstalter; München: Oldenbourg

Organismo Autónomo de Parques Nacionales (2005); Estudio para la planificación del uso público en el Parque Nacional de Garajonay; Monográfico sobre Turismo en la Isla de La Gomera; not published

Internet

ACANTUR (2005); homepage; <http://ecoturismocanarias.com/canarias/uk/islas.asp>; access: 08.04.2005 at 11.30

Autoridad portuaria de Santa Cruz / Tenerife; Consulta de tráfico;
<http://www.puertosdetenerife.org/OBJETO.ASP?a_obj=0&p_obj=44&obj=48>; access: 10.12.2004 at 14.50

Binter; Zona de prensa
<http://www.binternet.com/acercaMgr.php?opciones=6_8&referer=6_8&phpsessionid=7d5b96190e11f6d8e96b8cd5a362fa9e>; 05.03.05; 15.18

Caixa Catalunya (2005); Nuevas políticas para el turismo cultural; <http://obrasocial.caixacatalunya.es/osocial/main.html?idioma=2>; access: 30.03.05 at 11.30

Fred Olsen Lines (2005); Historia; <http://www.fredolsen.es/english/index2.htm>; access: 13.03.2005 at 17.15

N.A. (2004); A Baseline Definition of Culture; <http://www.wsu.edu:8001/vcwsu/commons/topics/culture/culture-definition.html>; access: 29.12.2004 at 22.45

Patronato de Turismo (2005); Historia; <http://www.gomera-island.com/inglesa/historia.htm>; access: 14.03.2005 at 13.30

VISIT (2004); Sustainable Indicators;
<www.netcoast.nl/coastlearn/website/tourism/tools_acc.htm>; access: 12.06.04 at 10.00

Other sources

ACANTUR (2005); Socios, Curso de Marketing para el Turismo Rural; <http://ecoturismocanarias.com>; access: 20.08.2005 at 19.30

Brown D.M. (ND); Rural Tourism, An annotated bibliography;
<http://www.nal.usda.gov/ric/ricpubs/rural_tourism.html>; access: 07.06.2004 at 20.30

Cabildo Insular (2005); Plan territorial especial de desarrollo turístico

Cabrini L. (2002); Turismo, desarrollo rural y sostenibilidad; Presentation of the European regional representative of the WTO at the VII Congress AECIT; 21.-23. October 2002

Expert Questionnaire (2005); Cuestionario sobre los aspectos sociales y culturales de La Gomera y los impactos turísticos; conducted by the author

Ideatur (2002); Reiseführer von La Gomera; 2nd edition, Santa Cruz de Tenerife: Graficas Tenerife

Workshop for DRP (2004); Diagnóstico Rural Participativo (PRA participative rural appraisal); 13th to 17th December 2004, San Sebastian, La Gomera

VDM publishing house ltd.

Scientific Publishing House

offers

free of charge publication

of current academic research papers, Bachelor's Theses, Master's Theses, Dissertations or Scientific Monographs

If you have written a thesis which satisfies high content as well as formal demands, and you are interested in a remunerated publication of your work, please send an e-mail with some initial information about yourself and your work to *info@vdm-publishing-house.com*.

Our editorial office will get in touch with you shortly.

VDM Publishing House Ltd.
Meldrum Court 17.
Beau Bassin
Mauritius
www.vdm-publishing-house.com

VDM Verlag Dr. Müller | LAP LAMBERT Academic Publishing | SVH Südwestdeutscher Verlag für Hochschulschriften